NATIONAL GEOGRAPHIC KiDS

ULTIMATE Explorer

FIELD GUIDE

Reptiles & Amphibians

Catherine Herbert Howell

NATIONAL GEOGRAPHIC
WASHINGTON, D.C.

Contents

**EASTERN PAINTED TURTLE,
PAGE 29**

**EASTERN COLLARED LIZARD,
PAGE 43**

**GREEN TREEFROG,
PAGE 140**

AMPHIBIANS

**ENSATINA,
PAGE 117**

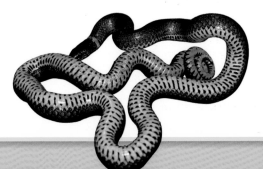

**RING-NECKED SNAKE,
PAGE 82**

MEETING
Reptiles and Amphibians

THE AMERICAN ALLIGATOR IS FAMOUS
FOR ITS "ALLIGATOR SMILE," BUT BE
SURE TO ADMIRE IT FROM A DISTANCE.

OUR WORLD IS FULL OF NATURAL WONDERS. Many of them are often overlooked because it takes extra effort to find them or because they're misunderstood. My favorite animals, reptiles and amphibians, qualify on both counts. They include some of nature's most fascinating creatures, but it takes time to find and appreciate them. People often don't understand them or know how to care for them, so many reptiles and amphibians are threatened or endangered.

Amphibians, such as salamanders and frogs, have been around for many millions of years, but today they are vulnerable to diseases and changes to their habitats. These changes are greater because humans are altering Earth's climate. Reptiles, which include crocodilians, turtles, lizards, and snakes, often are harmed by people who fear them or capture them for food or skins.

Most salamanders are secretive and hard to find, so you'll have to look carefully (but take care not to disturb their habitats). Frogs are mostly active at night, when they're hard to see—but frequently easy to hear. Archie Carr, an American biologist, said: "Frogs do for the night what birds do for the day ... they give it a voice. And that voice is a varied and stirring thing that ought to be better known."

Crocodilians can be frightening to humans, but they lavish their young with tender, loving care. Turtles often are portrayed as slow and clumsy movers, but many are immensely swift and graceful when they swim. Lizards dart about to catch insects and avoid predators. Snakes are quite elegant as they glide across the ground or climb a tree. All are best seen when they bask in the sun to warm their bodies.

So take this book and explore the out-of-doors near your home or during a vacation trip. Search for and begin to understand these animals. Marvel at their many wonderful adaptations, and appreciate them for the roles they play in nature.

—Robert Powell, Ph.D., Avila University

HOW TO USE This Book

THOUGH OFTEN QUITE SECRETIVE, reptiles and amphibians are out there—if you know where to find them. Take this book with you on your hunt to help you locate and identify reptiles and amphibians when you're exploring the outdoors.

Reptile or Amphibian Entry

HERE IS THE ANIMAL'S SCIENTIFIC NAME, ITS AVERAGE LENGTH, THE HABITATS IT LIVES IN, WHERE IT LIVES IN THE UNITED STATES AND CANADA, AND THE FOOD IT EATS.

THIS IS WHERE YOU'LL FIND THE REPTILE'S OR AMPHIBIAN'S COMMON NAME.

THIS TEXT GIVES YOU GENERAL INFORMATION ABOUT THE SPECIES, INCLUDING DETAILS ABOUT APPEARANCE AND KEY BEHAVIORS.

Hawksbill Sea Turtle

Eretmochelys imbricata LENGTH 30–35 in [75–90 cm] · HABITAT Coastal waters, bays, estuaries · RANGE Mainly tropical waters; seen on an Atlantic coast to Maine and on Pacific to Southern California · FOOD Sponges, jellyfish, other invertebrates, fish, algae

THE HAWKSBILL SEA TURTLE has a hawklike head and beak that can do major damage with a bite. This well-armored turtle has scutes, or bony plates, on its carapace that overlap, making it extra strong. As these turtles age, though, the scutes may pull apart and lie next to each other, making the carapace weaker. The Hawksbill's head has two protective scutes between the eyes. Female Hawksbills usually nest in tropical areas, but they sometimes come up onto Florida's Atlantic beaches to dig their nests and lay their clutches of about 140 eggs. The eggs hatch after 60 days and hatchlings make their risky dash to the sea.

DISCOVER A COOL FUN FACT OR SURPRISING BEHAVIOR ABOUT THIS SPECIES.

→ LOOK FOR THIS
Scientists have discovered three subspecies of **HAWKSBILL SEA TURTLES**: Atlantic, Pacific, and Indian Ocean Hawksbills. These creatures tend to hang out in shallow waters where sponges—one of their favorite foods—are abundant. Hawksbills can eat sponges that produce toxins without getting sick.

LEATHERY, BLACKISH CARAPACE

HAWKLIKE BEAK

2 SCUTES BETWEEN EYES

FLIPPERED FORELEGS

WEBBED HIND LEGS

10s

QUICKLY IDENTIFY A REPTILE OR AMPHIBIAN BY LOOKING FOR THESE BASIC FEATURES. CAN YOU NAME THE CORRECT SPECIES IN 10 SECONDS?

Laugh Out Loud! What kind of phone does a turtle use?

A shell phone.

REPTILE AND AMPHIBIAN JOKES, PUNS, AND RIDDLES WILL MAKE YOU AND YOUR FRIENDS LAUGH. TRY THEM ON YOUR FAMILY, TOO!

SPECIAL FEATURES CALLED REPTILE OR AMPHIB REPORTS give you an up-close look at reptile and amphibian appearance, their amazing behaviors, and their remarkable life cycles and lifestyles.

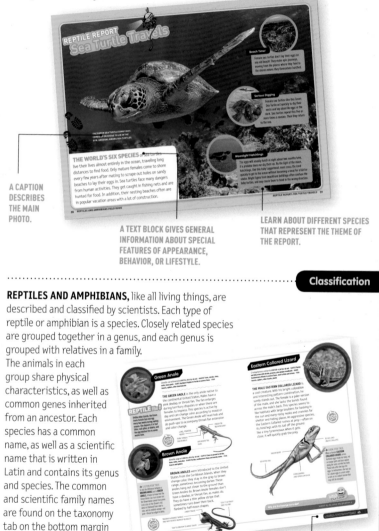

A CAPTION DESCRIBES THE MAIN PHOTO.

A TEXT BLOCK GIVES GENERAL INFORMATION ABOUT SPECIAL FEATURES OF APPEARANCE, BEHAVIOR, OR LIFESTYLE.

LEARN ABOUT DIFFERENT SPECIES THAT REPRESENT THE THEME OF THE REPORT.

REPTILES AND AMPHIBIANS, like all living things, are described and classified by scientists. Each type of reptile or amphibian is a species. Closely related species are grouped together in a genus, and each genus is grouped with relatives in a family.

The animals in each group share physical characteristics, as well as common genes inherited from an ancestor. Each species has a common name, as well as a scientific name that is written in Latin and contains its genus and species. The common and scientific family names are found on the taxonomy tab on the bottom margin of the pages.

TAXONOMY TAB

Reptiles and Amphibians

REPTILES AND AMPHIBIANS ARE VERTEBRATES (animals with backbones) that have been around for a long, long time.

WHAT'S THE STORY?

Reptiles and amphibians haven't changed much since they first appeared on Earth. Gnarly crocodilians, for example, resemble their ancestors from the Triassic period some 200 million years ago. Amphibians are old-timers, too. They appeared about 300 million years ago, when the first four-legged creatures left the water to walk on land. One, the *Eogyrinus*, or Dawn Tadpole, measured some 15 feet (4.6 m)!

Reptiles and amphibians are not very closely related, but scientists often group them together because they share some biological and ecological similarities. Amphibians are the older group, but by tradition reptiles are often listed first when the two groups are discussed.

Reptiles of the United States and Canada:

- Crocodilians (crocodiles and alligators)
- Turtles (including tortoises)
- Lizards
- Snakes

Amphibians include:

- Salamanders
- Frogs (including toads)

WHAT IS A REPTILE?

Reptiles are ectothermic—what some people call cold-blooded—which means they cannot control their body temperature internally. They have to bask in the sun to raise their body temperature. They spend a lot of time moving from sun to shade and also resting underground so they don't fry or freeze.

Watch for:

- Bodies usually covered with scales, shields, or bony plates
- Toes almost always with claws
- Most lay shelled eggs (some lizards and snakes give live birth).
- Young at birth can immediately move around and feed like adults.

Reptiles live in almost every kind of habitat in the United States and Canada except alpine tundra. Many are secretive and hard to find, even those that live near humans. Many are nocturnal—active mostly at night—and many burrow, spending a lot of time underground.

WHAT IS AN AMPHIBIAN?

Amphibians are also ectothermic. Unlike reptiles, amphibians have skin without scales and they breathe through their skin. They need to keep their skin moist, so they need to be near water. The name "amphibian" means "both [kinds of] life" and suggests that amphibians live at least part of their life in water.

Watch for:

- Smooth skin
- No claws
- Many species lay eggs in water. These hatch into aquatic larvae, or immature forms. Most larvae will transform into adults that live mainly on land.
- Some lay eggs in wet places on land. These species skip the larval stage in water.
- Some adults remain in their larval forms and continue to live in the water.

Amphibians live in many different kinds of habitats, as long as water is nearby. Some inhabit dry places but come out of the ground only when it rains.

PINE BARRENS TREEFROG

WHERE TO FIND THEM

Where do you go to find reptiles and amphibians? They're all around if you know where to look. They're even in urban areas like city parks, empty lots, and wooded yards.

Frogs and toads gather in the spring to breed in calm bodies of water, such as temporary pools that come from spring rains. Scientists call them vernal pools. "Vernal" means something that happens in the spring. At night you'll hear the mating calls of male frogs and toads trying to attract females.

Find out where frogs and toads gather in your area and ask a trusted adult to take you there after dark. Carry a flashlight and be sure not to step on any amphibians crossing the path or road! Often the noise will tell you where to look.

Visit a pond on a sunny day in spring or summer to see frogs, turtles, and snakes basking on rocks, logs, and banks. Approach the water slowly and quietly. You may see a stack of turtles perched on a log, a watersnake in a face-off with a frog, or a snake resting on a branch above.

Meadows are also a good place to find snakes. They often hide in the grass along trails used by rodents.

Salamanders are mainly woodland creatures that live under leaves, rocks, or logs or in slow-moving streams. Depending on where you live, you may

AMERICAN TOAD

see box turtles or ratsnakes as you hike through the woods.

In some places, a slow drive along a country road after a spring or summer rain is a good way to see lizards, snakes, and toads.

Many reptiles and amphibians leave tracks, but only on certain kinds of surfaces, such as fine dust, sand, and mud. An alligator leaves large, deep, clawed prints in mud. Many snakes might leave a smooth smudge in mud, while a Sidewinder will leave its signature J shape in sand (see page 79). Lizards may leave light footprints to the sides of a straight tail print. Slow-moving turtles leave a lot of clawed footprints close together, like the treads of a tank—with a long tail-drag line in between. Frogs and toads leave different kinds of prints, depending on whether they are hopping or walking.

SPOTTED SALAMANDER

PLAYING IT SAFE

You should avoid some kinds of reptiles. These include the crocodilians, venomous snakes, and some lizards, such as the Gila Monster. Also, never pick up a snapping turtle, even a small one. (They don't just snap, they clamp down really, really hard with their sharp-edged beaks!) Alligators are quite common in Louisiana and southern Florida, especially around lakes and canals. Look from a distance!

If your family is hiking in an area with venomous snakes, such as in the western mountains or the Southwestern desert, learn about the local snake species and know where to get medical help if you need it. Pay attention to what's on and beside the trail, especially in rocky areas. Never reach or poke a stick into a rock crevice to see if a reptile might be lurking there. Snakes, even venomous ones, would rather flee than fight. They're unlikely to strike unless they're surprised or feel threatened.

PROTECTING REPTILES AND AMPHIBIANS

Many reptile and amphibian species are vulnerable and declining in numbers. Numerous species are endangered.

All species of sea turtles are endangered. Stay away from beaches where they lay their eggs—and never disturb a nest. We owe sea turtles the best possible chance for their offspring to survive.

Land and pond turtles should be left alone. Native turtle species do not do well as pets. In fact, wild animals should never be kept as pets. It's very hard to meet their food and habitat needs in captivity. In places where turtles are still sold as pets, people often buy a turtle, put it in a plastic "habitat," and feed it lettuce, causing the turtle to get sick and die.

You should also leave frogs, salamanders, lizards, and snakes alone. They have complex nutritional, temperature, light, and moisture needs that only their natural habitats can provide.

Nature centers are great places to learn about the reptiles and amphibians in your area. By watching species there, you can recognize them more quickly in the field. You may also see a copperhead, rattlesnake, or other venomous snake safely at close range.

You can further help reptiles and amphibians by reminding adults not to use chemicals near bodies of water where reptiles or amphibians might live. Amphibians are especially sensitive to chemicals because they have porous skin that absorbs water—and any pollutants in it. Their bodies may develop extra limbs or show other abnormal features when water is polluted. It is also wise to never release any reptile or amphibian species that has been in captivity into nature. If you need to give up a captive animal of any kind, contact your local nature center or animal shelter for advice.

✓ CHECKLIST FOR FINDING REPTILES AND AMPHIBIANS
HERE ARE SOME THINGS TO BRING ALONG ON YOUR SEARCH FOR REPTILES AND AMPHIBIANS.

✓ **BINOCULARS**
Binoculars can help you see details of animals such as alligators from a safe distance. They also help you scan the landscape in a desert environment, for example, to look for the movement of snakes and lizards. Those large rocks far away may be a regular sunbathing site for local lizard species!

✓ **A GUIDE**
Take this book with you on hikes, bike rides, and car trips. You may also want to get a more focused guide that includes all the species in your area.

✓ **A NOTEBOOK**
Pack a small notebook and pen or pencil in your backpack. You'll want to keep a record of the species you see and when and where you find them. You can even make quick sketches that will help you identify them later.

✓ **PROPER CLOTHING**
Wear clothes that don't make you stick out in any habitat—earth colors of tan and green will likely blend well with your surroundings. Wear long pants, long sleeves, and sturdy shoes in woods, meadows, and tall grass to protect against poison ivy and ticks. Wear a hat for sun protection.

American Crocodile

Crocodylus acutus LENGTH 8–14 ft (2–4 m) · HABITAT Brackish and saltwater swamps · RANGE Southernmost Florida, including Everglades and Florida Keys · FOOD Fish, birds, frogs, mammals, invertebrates

SNOUT IS LONG AND TAPERED.

10s spotters

FOURTH TOOTH IN BOTTOM JAW VISIBLE WHEN MOUTH CLOSED

THE AMERICAN CROCODILE, like other crocodilians, has a signature look that hasn't changed much in 200 million years! Its long, V-shaped snout sets it apart from the American Alligator. Crocodiles are much rarer in the United States than alligators. They are found mainly in salt and brackish waters in southern Florida, especially from Miami southward. During breeding season, females lay their eggs in low mounds of sand. When the eggs hatch, the mother carries the mini-crocs carefully in her mouth to the water.

Spectacled Caiman

Caiman crocodilus LENGTH 4–8 ft (1–2 m) · HABITAT Freshwater marshes, ponds, and canals · RANGE Southern Florida, including Everglades · FOOD Fish, amphibians, birds, mammals, insects

A CURVED RIDGE OF BONE in front of its large eyes makes the Spectacled Caiman look like it's wearing glasses and distinguishes it from other crocodilians. This brownish, green, or yellowish species is native to Mexico and Central and South America. It came into the United States through the pet trade more than 60 years ago and either escaped or was released in southern Florida. Now the caiman competes for food and habitat with the American Alligator.

10s spotters

DARK BANDS ON TAIL

BONY RIDGE IN FRONT OF EYES

American Alligator

Alligator mississippiensis LENGTH 6–16 ft (2–5 m)
• HABITAT Freshwater and brackish marshes, swamps, bayous, and rivers • RANGE Coastal plain from southeastern Virginia to Florida, west to Texas • FOOD Fish, turtles, birds, snakes, mammals

THE AMERICAN ALLIGATOR is the largest native North American reptile. It can reach a length of 16 feet (5 m) and is an ancient species like its crocodile cousin. Alligators roam a large part of the coastal southeastern United States, often coming out of waterways and onto stream banks, lawns, and golf courses, where they may bask in the sun. In the water, alligators often float with only their eyes and nostrils above the surface, allowing them to scope out their next meal. At mating time, male alligators bellow loudly to announce their presence. Females build mounded nests, where they lay between 20 and 60 eggs.

BLACK TO BROWN TO GREEN ABOVE

YOUNG ARE DARK WITH YELLOW CROSSBANDS.

SNOUT IS BROAD AND ROUNDED.

PALE UNDERSIDE

10s. spotters

MAKE THIS!

EGG-CARTON ALLIGATOR

Round up: 1 cardboard egg carton, 2 toilet paper rolls, white construction paper, 2 googly eyes, green and red paint, glue.

1. Cut apart the top and bottom of the egg carton. Then cut off a third of the top half.
2. Cut the toilet paper rolls in half crosswise.
3. Paint the bottom of the egg carton and the third of the top green on the outside.
4. Paint the third of the top red on the inside (this is the bottom jaw).
5. Cut two jagged "tooth strips" from the construction paper. Fit them inside the top and bottom jaws.
6. Paint the toilet paper rolls green. Cut claw notches in the bottom of each. Now you have the legs.
7. Push the legs into the fourth and the last egg segments in the bottom half of the egg carton.
8. Bend back the bottom after the first three rows of segments to make the upper jaw.
9. Glue on the bottom jaw. Glue googly eyes on top, behind the upper jaw.

Eastern Snapping Turtle

Chelydra serpentina LENGTH 8–18 in (20–46 cm) • HABITAT Shallow freshwater and sometimes brackish water • RANGE Central and eastern U.S. to southern Canada • FOOD Invertebrates, fish, small mammals, carrion, plants

FOUND ON LAND or in fresh or brackish water, the aggressive Eastern Snapping Turtle snaps at the first sign of trouble. With a jaw that can clamp down with 1,000 pounds (454 kg) of pressure, this turtle can cause serious damage. It's no surprise that ambush is one strategy it uses to hunt food. The Snapper often buries itself in the muddy bottom of a pond with only its eyes and nostrils visible. It's able to snap quickly if prey comes near. But it also forages for the wide range of food it eats, including carrion and plant matter. As this turtle ages, its carapace (or shell) becomes smoother and may pick up a coating of algae.

DANGER!

If a Snapping Turtle of any kind ever crosses your path, DO NOT reach down to pick it up. This turtle has a very sharp beak set in a large, powerful jaw. You don't want to know what it feels like to have that beak clamp down on your finger!

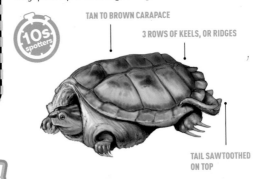

10s spotters

TAN TO BROWN CARAPACE

3 ROWS OF KEELS, OR RIDGES

TAIL SAWTOOTHED ON TOP

REPTILE file!

The Snapping Turtle has a large head, legs, and tail that keep it from being able to retreat very far into its shell for protection. But, no worries—its powerful snap can fend off most trouble.

Alligator Snapping Turtle

Macrochelys temminckii **LENGTH 15–26 in (38–66 cm)** ·
HABITAT Deep lakes and streams · **RANGE Alabama and the Florida
Panhandle, west to Texas, north to Kansas and Iowa** · **FOOD Fish, frogs,
mollusks, invertebrates, plants**

WITH ITS SCRUFFY HEAD and craggy
shell, the Alligator Snapping Turtle blends
in well on the muddy lake and stream
bottoms where it spends a lot of time. It
only needs to open its mouth and wiggle its
tongue—which looks like a worm—to attract
a fishy meal! The largest freshwater turtle in
North America, it can weigh up to 150 pounds
(68 kg). These turtles mate underwater.
Females head to land to dig a hole in the soil
and lay 20 to 50 round eggs. Two other species
of Alligator Snapping Turtles live in Georgia
and northern Florida.

→ LOOK FOR THIS
The range of the **ALLIGATOR
SNAPPING TURTLE** is smaller
than that of the Eastern Snapping
Turtle, but in areas where both
species are found, a few traits
help tell them apart. The Alligator
Snapping Turtle is up to twice as
large as the Eastern Snapping
Turtle and its sharp beak is more
hooked. It also has a pointier head.

HUGE HEAD

3 KEELS, OR RIDGES,
ON SHELL

10s
spotters

REPTILE file!

Because of its spiked shell,
beaklike jaws, and thick, scaled
tail, the Alligator Snapping
Turtle is often called the
"dinosaur of the turtle world."

HOOKED BEAK

What is a snapping turtle's favorite candy?

Jawbreakers!

Laugh
Out Loud!

Loggerhead Musk Turtle

Sternotherus minor LENGTH 3.5–5 in (9–13 cm) ▪ HABITAT Springs, streams, rivers, swamps, sinkholes ▪ RANGE Northern Georgia to northern Florida and southern Alabama ▪ FOOD Insects, snails, other invertebrates, plants

→ LOOK FOR THIS
To tell a **MUSK TURTLE** from the similar mud turtle, it helps to be able to see underneath it. The plastron, or bottom shell, of a musk turtle will have a single hinge instead of two. **LOGGERHEADS** also have barbels, thin points of flesh, on their chin. Eastern Musk Turtles have them on the chin and throat.

THE LOGGERHEAD MUSK TURTLE, as the name suggests, has an enormous head, which grows with age. The mouth has strong jaws used to crush the snails the turtle often eats. When a musk turtle is annoyed, it makes a stink, producing smelly musk from glands near its back legs. Even babies still in their eggshells can perform this stinky feat!

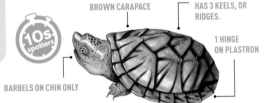

BROWN CARAPACE

CARAPACE OFTEN HAS 3 KEELS, OR RIDGES.

1 HINGE ON PLASTRON

BARBELS ON CHIN ONLY

Eastern Musk Turtle

Sternotherus odoratus LENGTH 2–4.5 in (5–11 cm) ▪ HABITAT Streams, ponds, lakes, canals, ditches ▪ RANGE Southern Canada and eastern U.S. to Wisconsin and Texas ▪ FOOD Insects, other invertebrates, tadpoles, fish, plants

WITH A NICKNAME OF STINKPOT, it's no surprise what the Eastern Musk Turtle does. It releases a nasty-smelling yellow fluid from glands under its carapace when it feels threatened or annoyed. You might miss seeing this turtle on the bottom of a stream. Its domed shell can pick up a blanket of algae that helps it blend in with stream stones.

2 LIGHT LINES ON HEAD

1 HINGE ON PLASTRON

BARBELS ON CHIN AND THROAT

Striped Mud Turtle

Kinosternon baurii LENGTH 3–4.75 in (8–12 cm) • HABITAT Swamps, ponds, canals, wet meadows • RANGE South Carolina to southern Florida • FOOD Insects, snails, algae, carrion, plants

THE SCUTES, OR BONY PLATES, that make up the top shell of the Striped Mud Turtle are almost see-through, making it possible to get a peek at the turtle's bony skeleton. This species roams quite far from water and is more land-based than other North American mud turtles. But it isn't too picky about where it finds its food. It will even search around for food, such as insects and their larvae, in a manure pile. Eww!

REPTILE file!

Two hinges are better than one for self-defense. The double hinges on the plastron, or bottom shell, of mud turtles enables the plastron to bend flexibly. This allows the turtle to securely tuck in its head, limbs, and tail, protecting itself from predators.

3 LONG, LIGHT STRIPES ON TOP

SMOOTH CARAPACE

2 HINGES ON PLASTRON

10s spotters

Yellow Mud Turtle

Kinosternon flavescens LENGTH 3.5–6 in (9–15 cm) • HABITAT Streams, rivers, ponds, lakes • RANGE South-central U.S.; separate populations in Illinois and Iowa • FOOD Insects, worms, snails, tadpoles, plants

THE POPULATION OF YELLOW MUD TURTLES in the United States is shrinking because of loss of its habitat due to construction. The species is now considered endangered in a number of states. Its natural habitat is freshwater with a muddy bottom, but it will travel long distances—especially in times of drought—to reach a water source, even an artificial one, such as a livestock watering tank. This shy species also appears on land during rains and will hunker down under leaves and brush in cool weather.

SMOOTH OLIVE TO BROWN CARAPACE

10s spotters

DARK-OUTLINED SCUTES

YELLOW ON CHIN AND THROAT

Eastern Mud Turtle

Kinosternon subrubrum **LENGTH** 3–4 in (8–10 cm) · **HABITAT** Marshes, ponds, swamps, other wetlands · **RANGE** South-central and eastern U.S. south from Long Island · **FOOD** Worms, larvae, other invertebrates, fish, plants

THE EASTERN MUD TURTLE has more habitat options than other mud turtle species. It can live in fresh and brackish water, as well as in coastal waters and on islands. It may wander far on land in search of a wide range of food, from worms to plants. At breeding time, females dig nests in loose soil that doesn't get soggy when it rains and is dense with vegetation for cover. There they deposit up to six oval-shaped, pinkish or bluish eggs with hard shells. They may do this up to three separate times in one season. Sometimes the females make their nests in the lodges of American Beavers or Muskrats—sometimes when the mammals still live in other parts of the lodge. The turtle hatchlings emerge in about 10 weeks.

→ LOOK FOR THIS
You can tell **MUD** and **MUSK** turtles apart by looking at their plastrons (bottom shells). **MUD TURTLES** have large plastrons with two hinges. **MUSK TURTLES** have smaller plastrons with one hinge.

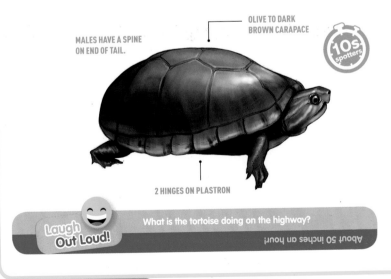

MALES HAVE A SPINE ON END OF TAIL.

OLIVE TO DARK BROWN CARAPACE

10s spotters

2 HINGES ON PLASTRON

Laugh Out Loud!
What is the tortoise doing on the highway?
About 50 inches an hour!

Northwestern Pond Turtle

Actinemys marmorata LENGTH 3.5–8.5 in (9–22 cm) • HABITAT Marshes, swamps, ponds, lakes, rivers • RANGE Washington State to California; separate population in Nevada • FOOD Fish, frogs, aquatic plants, carrion

THE WESTERN POND TURTLE keeps a lower profile than other pond turtles. Its carapace lacks the dome shape of many pond turtle species. This water-loving turtle likes a wet habitat with lots of aquatic plants. It also likes to climb up on a log or bank to soak up the sun's warming rays. With an open mouth to make it look threatening, it will stare down a rival that shows up to claim the same spot.

REPTILE file!

The female **NORTHWESTERN POND TURTLE** nests any time from April through August, depending on where she lives. She seeks out a sunny spot to dig a nest for the 3 to 14 eggs she will lay. The baby turtles hatch in about three months.

OLIVE TO BROWN CARAPACE

CARAPACE MAY HAVE DARK LINES OR YELLOW SPOTS.

10s spotters

Spotted Turtle

Clemmys guttata LENGTH 3.5–4.5 in (9–11 cm) • HABITAT Shallow streams, wet meadows, woodlands, bogs, beaver ponds • RANGE East Coast from southern Maine to Florida, Great Lakes region, upper Ohio River • FOOD Insects, other invertebrates, frogs, carrion

THE SPOTTED TURTLE'S randomly located spots look like they were flicked on from a paint-filled brush. The spots camouflage it in dense vegetation. A very social turtle, it is seen in groups with Bog Turtles and other species. The Spottie is pretty laid-back. If you disturb one while it basks in the sun, it will ease itself back into the water without hurrying.

10s spotters

YELLOW SPOTS ON CARAPACE

MALE HAS BROWN EYES.

FEMALE HAS ORANGE EYES.

Wood Turtle

Glyptemys insculpta LENGTH 5–8 in (13–20 cm) ◦ HABITAT Woodland streams, swamps, marshes, farmland ◦ RANGE Nova Scotia, Canada, to Minnesota, south to Virginia and West Virginia ◦ FOOD Invertebrates, tadpoles, fruit

CARAPACE
SEGMENTS
FORM RIDGED
PYRAMIDS.

NECK AND FORELEGS
ARE OFTEN ORANGE.

BROWN CARAPACE

ONE OF THE MOST TERRESTRIAL (land-dwelling) turtle species, next to tortoises and box turtles, the Wood Turtle seems to carry a tray of ridged pyramids on its back. Even though it lives on land, the Wood Turtle spends a lot of time in water. But its searches for food may take it far from water. It may head to a recently plowed field, where it forages for worms and insects in the turned-over soil.

Ornate Box Turtle

Terrapene ornata LENGTH 4–5 in (10–13 cm) ◦ HABITAT Prairie, plains, pastures, open woods, sandy areas ◦ RANGE Mid-central and south-central U.S. to Southeast ◦ FOOD Insects, worms, berries, small vertebrates, carrion

WITH YELLOW LINES that spread from a central point on the carapace, the Ornate Box Turtle's pattern is more defined than those of other box turtles. This turtle has a bad attitude, becoming aggressive when disturbed. Though it eats berries, it prefers to eat insects and small vertebrates. This species tolerates hot and dry environments, burrowing into sand or dirt to escape the warmest part of the day.

HIGH-DOMED CARAPACE
WITH YELLOW LINES
EXTENDING FROM CENTER

HINGED PLASTRON HAS SIMILAR MARKINGS AS CARAPACE.

Eastern Box Turtle

Terrapene carolina **LENGTH** 4.5–6 in (11–15 cm) • **HABITAT**
Woodlands, meadows, pastures, other open areas • **RANGE** Eastern U.S.
from southern Maine south to Florida, west to the Mississippi River •
FOOD Fruit, flowers, vegetables, insects, worms, slugs

WHEN SOMEONE SAYS "TURTLE," many
people immediately think of the Eastern
Box Turtle. What's not to love about this
woodland icon, with its high-domed shell; thick,
stubby legs; and beaked head? And don't forget
its alert, beady eyes—orange in males, yellow
in females. This turtle has a built-in defense
system that protects it from most kinds of
predators. When feeling threatened, the Eastern
Box can hole up in its shell, drawing in its head
and limbs completely and clamping up tightly,
thanks to a flexible, hinged plastron, or bottom
shell. Though it seems very tortoise-like, the
Eastern Box is more closely related to water
turtles and often takes a good, long soak in a
pond or puddle.

REPTILE file !

To make a meal of a sealed-up
box turtle, a Great Horned Owl
will sometimes carry a turtle
into the air with its talons.
Then it drops the turtle onto
rocks to crack the shell and
get to the soft parts.

10s spotters

CARAPACE MAY HAVE YELLOW,
ORANGE, OR OLIVE MARKINGS.

HIGH-DOMED CARAPACE
IS TAN, BROWN, OR BLACK.

MALE HAS ORANGE
EYES, FEMALE
HAS YELLOW.

BEAKED UPPER JAW

EXPERT'S CIRCLE

DON'T BE FOOLED A close relative of the Eastern Box Turtle, the
THREE-TOED BOX TURTLE (*Terrapene carolina triunguis*) usually has three toes on its hind feet.
It also has orange or yellow patches on its head and front legs.

Diamond-backed Terrapin

Malaclemys terrapin LENGTH 4–5.5 in (10–14 cm) • HABITAT Salt marshes, tidal flats, other brackish and salt waters • RANGE Atlantic and Gulf Coasts from Cape Cod to Texas • FOOD Crustaceans, other invertebrates, fish

BEFORE MANY STATES listed it as endangered or threatened, the Diamond-backed Terrapin often was hunted for food. In addition to hunting, the development of land along coasts also threatens this turtle's existence by destroying its habitat. Climate change is another threat. If the level of the seas continues to rise, the water the turtles live in could become too salty for their survival. The Diamond-back has a spotted head and limbs, and the scutes, or plates, of its carapace show rings added as the turtle grows. Female Diamond-backs can measure up to twice as long as males. After mating, the female digs a hole on the beach away from the water's reach and lays 4 to 18 leathery eggs. The eggs will hatch in two to four months.

→ **LOOK FOR THIS**
Seven different kinds of **DIAMOND-BACKS** live along the Atlantic and Gulf Coasts. They look pretty similar from above, but the color and pattern of their plastrons are quite different.

10s spotters

HEAD AND SIDES ARE SPOTTED.

SCUTES HAVE GROWTH RINGS.

BROWN OR BLACK KEELED CARAPACE

YELLOWISH OR GREENISH PLASTRON

REPTILE file!

The word "terrapin" comes from an Algonquin Indian word for "the turtle." In the 1930s, the University of Maryland chose the Diamond-backed Terrapin for its mascot. It calls its representative reptile Testudo. A statue of Testudo stands in front of the main library at the university.

Northern Map Turtle

Graptemys geographica LENGTH 3.5–6.25 in (9–16 cm) • HABITAT Rivers, lakes • RANGE Great Lakes area to Tennessee and Alabama; Arkansas and Missouri River areas • FOOD Insects, crayfish, snails, mollusks

THE NORTHERN MAP TURTLE wears colorful patterns on its body and shell. This turtle's head has a series of yellow lines that look like the lines that show how high the land is on a map. Dark lines on the carapace resemble the way maps depict waterways. Female Northern Map Turtles can grow to be more than twice as long as males, with bigger heads and larger jaws. The female can crush larger clams and other shelled animals with her supersize jaws.

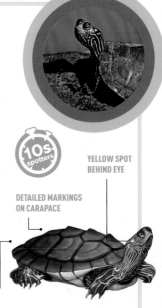

YELLOW SPOT BEHIND EYE

DETAILED MARKINGS ON CARAPACE

LOW CARAPACE WITH KEEL (RIDGE)

Black-knobbed Map Turtle

Graptemys nigrinoda LENGTH 3–4.5 in (8–11 cm) • HABITAT Streams and rivers • RANGE Southern rivers and their tributaries • FOOD Insects, other invertebrates

BLACK-KNOBBED MAP TURTLES have a lot of different features on their shell. Knoblike structures sit at the top of the carapace, making the turtle look kind of like a *Stegosaurus*. Sharp edges line the rim of the carapace, a feature that could have contributed to the alternate common name, Black-knobbed Sawback. Black-knobbed Map Turtles make their home in southern rivers and their tributaries.

OLIVE-BROWN CARAPACE

BLACK, KNOBLIKE STRUCTURES ALONG BACK

YELLOW MARK BEHIND EYE

False Map Turtle

Graptemys pseudogeographica **LENGTH 3.5–5.75 in (9–15 cm)**
HABITAT Rivers, lakes, ponds, bayous, marshes ▪ **RANGE** Waters of
Missouri–Mississippi River system ▪ **FOOD** Mollusks, insects, dead fish

FALSE MAP TURTLES like to live in bodies of water with lots of aquatic plants and squishy, muddy bottoms. When they want to bask—or catch some rays—they often climb up steep riverbanks to get to spots where few other turtles care to go. In the winter, they take shelter in riverbank burrows or they move into muskrat lodges—sometimes sharing them with the muskrats. In the southern parts of their range, they often remain active during the winter months. Water pollution, the rerouting of river channels, and the buildup of silt from erosion are some of the reasons False Map Turtle populations—and the populations of other turtle species—are declining.

REPTILE file!

Like female Northern Map Turtles, female False Map Turtles grow up to twice as long as males. They make the most of breeding season by laying up to four clutches of about 14 eggs each in nests they dig in sandy banks.

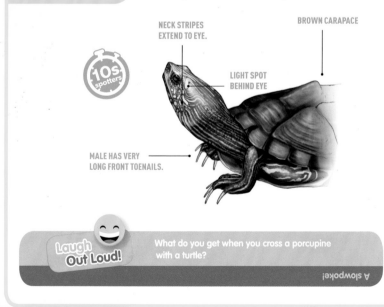

NECK STRIPES EXTEND TO EYE.

BROWN CARAPACE

LIGHT SPOT BEHIND EYE

MALE HAS VERY LONG FRONT TOENAILS.

10s spotters

Laugh Out Loud!
What do you get when you cross a porcupine with a turtle?

A slowpoke!

Red-eared Slider

Trachemys scripta elegans LENGTH 5–8 in (13–20 cm) • HABITAT Quiet rivers, streams, swamps, ponds, lakes • RANGE West Virginia to New Mexico, south to Gulf of Mexico • FOOD Plants, invertebrates, fish, tadpoles

A RED-EARED SLIDER doesn't actually have ears. Instead, a long, stretched oval extends back from the eye where you'd expect an ear to be in many—but not all—members of this species. Red-ears and other pond sliders are the most common North American turtle, preferring shallow, quiet waters with muddy bottoms. The shell patterns, head, limbs, and tail of Red-eared Sliders usually darken with age.

CARAPACE HAS YELLOW STREAKS AND BARS.

RED STRIPES ON HEAD

PLASTRON IS YELLOW WITH DARK BLOTCHES.

Yellow-bellied Slider

Trachemys scripta scripta LENGTH 5–8 in (13–20 cm) • HABITAT Ponds, streams. swamps, lakes, rivers • RANGE Southeastern Virginia to northern Florida, west to Texas • FOOD Insects, small fish, tadpoles, frogs, plants

THE YELLOW-BELLIED SLIDER, like most slider turtles, is kind of a beach bum. On a mild, sunny day in the spring and fall, it will bask for hours in the sunshine. This is really a combo land-and-water species. In the winter, Yellow-bellies leave the water to brumate, or hibernate, on land. The yellow marks on the sides of the head are more noticeable on females and young. The shell of an adult male may turn very dark with age.

YELLOW MARK ON SIDES OF HEAD

ROUNDED LOWER JAW

PLASTRON IS YELLOW, WITH CIRCULAR MARKS IN FRONT.

CARAPACE IS BROWN OR OLIVE.

River Cooter

Pseudemys concinna LENGTH 7–13 in (18–33 cm) • HABITAT Streams, rivers, lakes, swamps, marshes • RANGE Coastal plains from Virginia to Georgia and Alabama • FOOD Aquatic plants, berries, insects, fish, carrion

REPTILE file!

The name "cooter" probably comes from an African word, *kuta*, which means "turtle." The River Cooter once served as a common—and abundant— food source in the South.

RIVER COOTERS like to hang with Painted Turtles and sliders. You often can find all three resting on a single log, basking together in the sun. At the first sign of trouble though, the River Cooter will plunge into the water. A good swimmer, the species can hold its own against strong currents in rivers and streams.

BROWN CARAPACE

CARAPACE OFTEN HAS CONCENTRIC (CIRCLES INSIDE CIRCLES) MARKINGS.

MALES HAVE LONG FRONT CLAWS.

10s spotters

Northern Red-bellied Cooter

Pseudemys rubriventris LENGTH 10–12 in (25–30 cm) • HABITAT Ponds, lakes, streams, rivers, marshes • RANGE Southern New Jersey to northeastern North Carolina • FOOD Aquatic plants, invertebrates, tadpoles

ALSO KNOWN AS THE RED-BELLIED TURTLE, the Northern Red-bellied Cooter lurks in deeper water than many other basking turtles. It's usually larger than other cooters, too. When sunning itself on a log or stream bank, it slides into the water at the slightest disturbance. Male Northern Red-bellies have the long front claws typical of cooters. A separate population of this species lives in southeastern Massachusetts.

10s spotters

RED BARS ON CARAPACE

REDDISH PLASTRON

MALE HAS ELONGATED FRONT CLAWS.

Eastern Painted Turtle

Chrysemys picta picta LENGTH 3.5–7 in (9–18 cm) • HABITAT
Sluggish, shallow streams; rivers; lakes • RANGE **U.S.–Canada border
to Nova Scotia, northern and south-central U.S.** • FOOD **Aquatic plants,
invertebrates**

TAKE A BASIC BASKING TURTLE, add
some bright markings on its head, limbs,
and shell—including a colorful and fancy
plastron, or lower shell—and you've got an
Eastern Painted Turtle. The species is abundant
and has the widest range of all North American
turtles. Females, which often are larger than
males, may lay up to four clutches a year, each
clutch containing 2 to 20 oval eggs. Like many
other young turtles, painted turtles start out
as carnivores (meat-eaters) and transition to
herbivores (plant-eaters) as they age. Three
subspecies of painted turtles have clear
differences in pattern, except where their
ranges overlap. In those places, you can find
individuals that show characteristics of more
than one kind of painted turtle.

→ LOOK FOR THIS
PAINTED TURTLES spend the
winter in the same place they
spend their active season—the
water. They rest under logs
or stumps underwater or
sometimes find some space in
a beaver or muskrat lodge—
maybe even sharing the space
with these animals.

YELLOW LINES
ON HEAD

RED PATTERN ON
EDGE OF CARAPACE

DECORATED YELLOW PLASTRON

STRIPED LEGS
AND TAIL

Where do turtles keep their money?

In a river bank!

Laugh Out Loud!

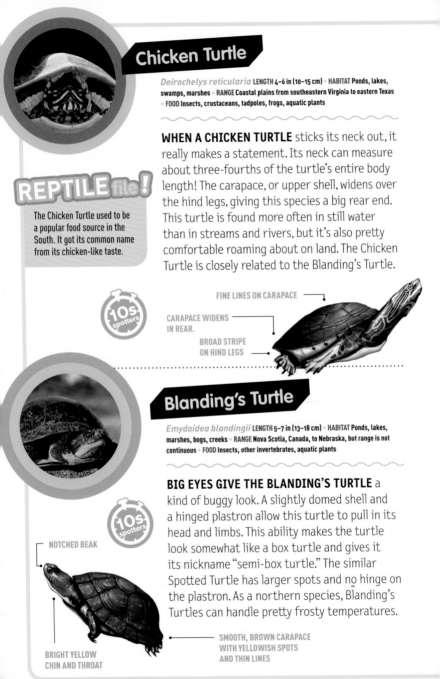

Chicken Turtle

Deirochelys reticularia LENGTH 4–6 in (10–15 cm) ◦ HABITAT Ponds, lakes, swamps, marshes ◦ RANGE Coastal plains from southeastern Virginia to eastern Texas ◦ FOOD Insects, crustaceans, tadpoles, frogs, aquatic plants

REPTILE file!

The Chicken Turtle used to be a popular food source in the South. It got its common name from its chicken-like taste.

WHEN A CHICKEN TURTLE sticks its neck out, it really makes a statement. Its neck can measure about three-fourths of the turtle's entire body length! The carapace, or upper shell, widens over the hind legs, giving this species a big rear end. This turtle is found more often in still water than in streams and rivers, but it's also pretty comfortable roaming about on land. The Chicken Turtle is closely related to the Blanding's Turtle.

10s spotters

FINE LINES ON CARAPACE

CARAPACE WIDENS IN REAR.

BROAD STRIPE ON HIND LEGS

Blanding's Turtle

Emydoidea blandingii LENGTH 5–7 in (13–18 cm) ◦ HABITAT Ponds, lakes, marshes, bogs, creeks ◦ RANGE Nova Scotia, Canada, to Nebraska, but range is not continuous ◦ FOOD Insects, other invertebrates, aquatic plants

BIG EYES GIVE THE BLANDING'S TURTLE a kind of buggy look. A slightly domed shell and a hinged plastron allow this turtle to pull in its head and limbs. This ability makes the turtle look somewhat like a box turtle and gives it its nickname "semi-box turtle." The similar Spotted Turtle has larger spots and no hinge on the plastron. As a northern species, Blanding's Turtles can handle pretty frosty temperatures.

10s spotters

NOTCHED BEAK

BRIGHT YELLOW CHIN AND THROAT

SMOOTH, BROWN CARAPACE WITH YELLOWISH SPOTS AND THIN LINES

Mojave Desert Tortoise

Gopherus agassizii LENGTH 8–15 in (20–38 cm) ▪ HABITAT Canyons, slopes, dunes, washes, oases ▪ RANGE Desert areas of southern California, Nevada, Utah, Arizona ▪ FOOD Grasses, herbs, cacti

DO YOU KNOW WHY the Mojave Desert Tortoise has the genus name of *Gopherus*? If you guess that this tortoise—and others in the same genus—are named for the gopher, the burrowing rodent, you're right! These tortoises use their scaly, flattened forelimbs to dig burrows in sand that's not very loose. In contrast, their rear limbs are round and stumpy. This desert species gets a lot of the water it needs from the plants it eats.

GROWTH RINGS ON EACH SCUTE, OR PLATE

HIGH-DOMED CARAPACE

PLASTRON COMES UP UNDER CHIN IN MALES.

Gopher Tortoise

Gopherus polyphemus LENGTH 6–9.5 in (15–24 cm) ▪ HABITAT Sandy areas between grasslands and forests ▪ RANGE Southwestern South Carolina to Florida and eastern Louisiana ▪ FOOD Grasses, other plants, berries

THE MASTER BUILDER of the reptile world, the Gopher Tortoise provides housing for up to 300 other species when it excavates a burrow for itself. Animals such as Burrowing Owls, snakes, and invertebrates shelter in the turtle's tunnels, which are especially important in places where there's a lot of human housing development and limited space for animals. This species grazes calmly on grasses and other plants, earning the nickname "cow with a shell."

SCUTES, OR PLATES, HAVE A PATTERN OF CIRCLES INSIDE CIRCLES.

TAN TO BROWN DOMED CARAPACE

MALE'S PLASTRON BENDS UP UNDER CHIN.

Loggerhead Sea Turtle

Caretta caretta LENGTH 31–47 in (79–120 cm) • HABITAT Oceans, bays, estuaries, tidal rivers • RANGE All oceans, nests regularly on Atlantic coast as far north as North Carolina • FOOD Marine invertebrates, fish, algae

THE LOGGERHEAD SEA TURTLE lives at sea most of its life. It moves its flippered forelegs in a figure-eight stroke to swim. Its webbed hind legs work as rudders. When it's young, the turtle stays mostly far out at sea, but it moves closer to the coastline as it ages. It takes up to 25 years for these turtles to be able to reproduce. The females come onto land every two or three years to lay eggs in nests they dig on beaches at night. They do this every few weeks for several months and then head back out to sea. The hatchlings are on their own when they leave the nest. They must avoid birds and other predators to reach the water.

save the turtles!

Sea turtles need help. Even though many countries protect nesting sea turtles, their future is threatened because they are still captured illegally, caught in fishing nets, and have to share their nesting beaches with hotels and condos. Learn how you can help them at defenders.org/publication/five-things-you-can-do-save-sea-turtles.

MASSIVE HEAD WITH STRONG JAWS

SHELL IS REDDISH BROWN.

FLIPPERED FORELEGS

WEBBED HIND LEGS

10s spotters

Laugh Out Loud! What kind of photos do turtles take?

Shellfies!

Green Sea Turtle

Chelonia mydas LENGTH 36–48 in (90–120 cm) ▪ HABITAT Oceans, bays, estuaries ▪ RANGE Warm waters of Atlantic and Pacific Oceans ▪ FOOD Algae, sea grasses, marine invertebrates

THE GREEN SEA TURTLE looks brown overall, so how does it get its name? The "green" refers to the color of its body fat. These turtles, now endangered, have long been prized as a food source and are still hunted despite their protected status. Female Green Sea Turtles make journeys of thousands of miles from the sea grass "pastures" where they graze to the beaches where they lay their eggs. The females commonly lay clutches of about 100 or more eggs in the sand. The eggs hatch in about two months. Like all newly hatched sea turtles, they must reach the sea quickly to avoid being eaten.

REPTILE file!

Young Green Sea Turtles don't graze much on sea grasses like adults do. Instead, they like to munch on marine invertebrates like crabs, sponges, and jellyfish.

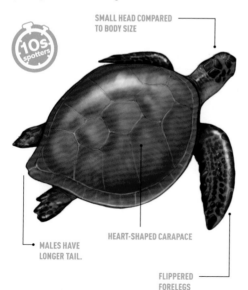

SMALL HEAD COMPARED TO BODY SIZE

MALES HAVE LONGER TAIL.

HEART-SHAPED CARAPACE

FLIPPERED FORELEGS

save the turtles!

Green Sea Turtles suffer from a disease that causes soft-tissue growths. If the growths are on the outside, they make it hard for the turtle to move freely. Internal growths harm organs. Scientists don't know what causes the disease, but it often happens near areas where lots of people live, so pollution could be a cause.

Hawksbill Sea Turtle

Eretmochelys imbricata LENGTH 30–35 in (75–90 cm) · HABITAT Coastal waters, bays, estuaries · RANGE Mainly tropical waters; seen on Atlantic coast to Maine and on Pacific to Southern California · FOOD Sponges, jellyfish, other invertebrates, fish, algae

THE HAWKSBILL SEA TURTLE has a hawklike head and beak that can do major damage with a bite. This well-armored turtle has scutes, or bony plates, on its carapace that overlap, making it extra strong. As these turtles age, though, the scutes may pull apart and lie next to each other, making the carapace weaker. The Hawksbill's head has two protective scutes between the eyes. Female Hawksbills usually nest in tropical areas, but they sometimes come up onto Florida's Atlantic beaches to dig their nests and lay their clutches of about 140 eggs. The eggs hatch after 60 days and hatchlings make their risky dash to the sea.

→ **LOOK FOR THIS**
Scientists have discovered three subspecies of **HAWKSBILL SEA TURTLES**: Atlantic, Pacific, and Indian Ocean Hawksbills. These creatures tend to hang out in shallow waters where sponges—one of their favorite foods—are abundant. Hawksbills can eat sponges that produce toxins without getting sick.

LEATHERY, BLACKISH CARAPACE

HAWKLIKE BEAK

2 SCUTES BETWEEN EYES

FLIPPERED FORELEGS

WEBBED HIND LEGS

10s spotters

Laugh Out Loud! What kind of phone does a turtle use?

A shell phone!

Kemp's Ridley Sea Turtle

Lepidochelys kempii LENGTH 23.5–27.5 in (60–70 cm) • HABITAT Shallow
coastal waters • RANGE Gulf of Mexico; sometimes as far north as Nova Scotia, Canada
• FOOD Crabs, other marine invertebrates, fish

A SHELL AS LONG AS IT IS WIDE gives the
Kemp's Ridley Sea Turtle a kind of swimming
Frisbee look. The Kemp's Ridley is the smallest
and rarest sea turtle species. It used to gather
in the tens of thousands in the Gulf of Mexico
during mating season. The females would then
come ashore by the thousands in the daytime to
lay their 100 sphere-shaped eggs in a nest dug
into the sand. These gatherings are known as
arribadas, from the Spanish word for "arrivals."
Kemp's Ridley numbers are falling due to things
like pollution, loss of nesting habitat, and
climate change.

10s spotters

GRAY OR
GREEN
CARAPACE

YELLOWISH
PLASTRON

Olive Ridley Sea Turtle

Lepidochelys olivacea LENGTH 24–30 in (60–76 cm) • HABITAT Warm oceans
RANGE Southern Atlantic and Pacific Oceans • FOOD Jellyfish, snails, crabs, algae

A COUSIN of the Kemp's Ridley Sea Turtle,
the Olive Ridley Sea Turtle roams the warmer,
deeper waters of the southern oceans. Olive
Ridleys start out gray in color, turning olive
green over time. They're considered the most
abundant sea turtle but are still listed as
endangered. That just shows the risky status
of the world's marine turtles. The Olive Ridley
is also known as the Pacific Ridley Sea Turtle.

10s spotters

1 OR 2 CLAWS
ON FLIPPERS

OLIVE GREEN,
HEART-SHAPED CARAPACE

Leatherback Sea Turtle

Dermochelys coriacea LENGTH 50–70 in (120–170 cm) ▪ HABITAT Oceans ▪ RANGE Atlantic and Pacific Oceans; nests along Atlantic as far north as North Carolina ▪ FOOD Jellyfish, other marine invertebrates

THE LEATHERBACK SEA TURTLE is the largest turtle species in the world. One record breaker measured more than nine feet (2.7 m) and weighed more than 2,000 pounds (907 kg). That's longer than an NBA player is tall and as heavy as a small car! Leatherbacks travel through the ocean, looking for lots of the jellyfish and other marine invertebrates they eat. The species can catch slimy jellyfish because its mouth contains long spines to nab them. The jellyfish's stinging cells don't seem to bother the leatherback. These turtles represent the last members of a turtle family that goes back more than 100 million years, to the time of the dinosaurs.

REPTILE file!

The female Leatherback swims thousands of miles back to the beach where she hatched to lay her own eggs. She makes the amazing journey every two or three years. To make the most of her extreme efforts—and ensure that some of her offspring survive—she lays multiple clutches of 50 to 170 eggs during each breeding period.

→ **LOOK FOR THIS**
LEATHERBACK SEA TURTLES, as their name suggests, lack the typical hard, bony shells of other turtle species. Instead, the Leatherback carapace is flexible and feels almost rubbery. Ridges on the carapace give it a streamlined shape that helps the turtle swim easily on long ocean journeys.

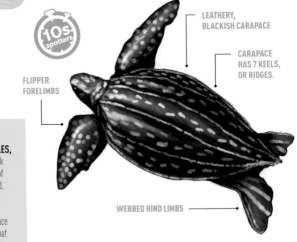

10s. spotters

LEATHERY, BLACKISH CARAPACE

CARAPACE HAS 7 KEELS, OR RIDGES.

FLIPPER FORELIMBS

WEBBED HIND LIMBS

Smooth Softshell

Apalone mutica LENGTH 4.5–7 in (11–18 cm) ◦ HABITAT Rivers, streams ◦ RANGE Drainage areas of major rivers in central U.S. ◦ FOOD Crayfish, other invertebrates, frogs, fish

SMOOTH SOFTSHELL TURTLES don't really have soft shells. Underneath a covering of soft, leathery skin—similar to a pancake—is the same bony shell that hard-shelled turtles have. Softshells just lack the plates, called scutes, that cover the undershells of hard-shelled turtles. This is what makes them softer. Because they're softer and more likely to be eaten, Softshells have sharp beaks and claws for protection. They are speedy on land and in water, which also helps them stay safe. Females are up to twice as long as males.

LONG SNOUT

LEATHERY, PANCAKE-LIKE CARAPACE

Spiny Softshell

Apalone spinifera LENGTH 4.5–7 in (11–18 cm) ◦ HABITAT Creeks, ponds, lakes, rivers ◦ RANGE Central and southeastern U.S. ◦ FOOD Fish, frogs, crayfish, other invertebrates

LONG SNOUT

SMALL SPINES ON THE FRONT EDGE of its carapace help you tell the difference between a Spiny and a Smooth Softshell. This very aquatic turtle never strays too far from water, and while it is submerged, it uses its snorkel-like snout to breathe at the surface. Female Spinys are larger than males. They also have dark blotches on their flat carapaces, whereas males have black-bordered spots.

LONG NECK

SMALL SPINES ON FRONT OF CARAPACE

Sea Turtle Travels

THE GREEN SEA TURTLE SOMETIMES COMES UP ON SHORE TO LIE IN THE SUN, UNUSUAL AMONG SEA TURTLES.

THE WORLD'S SIX SPECIES of sea turtles live their lives almost entirely in the ocean, traveling long distances to find food. Only mature females come to shore every few years after mating to scrape out holes on sandy beaches to lay their eggs in. Sea turtles face many dangers from human activities. They get caught in fishing nets and are hunted for food. In addition, their nesting beaches often are in popular vacation areas with a lot of construction.

Beach Time!

Female sea turtles don't lay their eggs on any old beach! They make epic journeys, moving from the places where they feed to the shores where they themselves hatched.

Serious Digging

Female sea turtles like this Green Sea Turtle act quickly to dig their nests and lay about 80 eggs in the dark. Sea turtles repeat this five or more times a season. Then they return to the sea.

Moonlight Hatchlings

The eggs will usually hatch at night about two months later, if a predator does not dig them up. By the light of the moon, hatchlings, like this baby Loggerhead, must cross the sand quickly to get to the ocean without becoming a meal for a bird or snake. Bright lights from beachfront buildings often confuse the baby turtles, and may cause them to head in the wrong direction.

Western Banded Gecko

Coleonyx variegatus LENGTH 4.5–6 in (11–15 cm) • HABITAT **Arid rocky areas, canyons, dunes** • RANGE **Southeastern California into Nevada, Utah, Arizona, New Mexico** • FOOD **Insects, spiders**

THE WESTERN BANDED GECKO hides among rocks or under logs or brush during the hottest part of desert days. Unlike other geckos that have eyelids that don't move, the Western Banded has eyelids that open and shut, concealing bulging eyeballs with vertical pupils. It also lacks the toe pads that other geckos have. This species hunts at night, waving its tail as it stalks insects and spiders.

BROWN BANDS ON BODY AND TAIL

VERY BULGY EYES

SLENDER TOES WITHOUT PADS

Reef Gecko

Sphaerodactylus notatus LENGTH 2–2.25 in (5–6 cm) • HABITAT **Pinelands, vacant lots, gardens** • RANGE **Southern Florida** • FOOD **Small insects, spiders**

THE REEF GECKO IS TINY. It's only about two inches (5 cm) long, including its tail. This species is the only native gecko that lives east of the Mississippi River. It's difficult to spot the shy and secretive creature unless you turn over leaf litter around dusk, when these little critters are active. Because of their size, it's not a surprise that females lay only a single egg at a time. A hatchling can measure half the size of an adult.

FEMALES HAVE 3 LINES ON HEAD.

LARGE SCALES FOR SIZE OF BODY

BROWN BODY COVERED WITH DARK SPOTS

Madagascan Day Gecko

Phelsuma grandis LENGTH 10–12 in (25–30 cm) ▪ HABITAT Trees ▪ RANGE Introduced into Florida ▪ FOOD Insects, other invertebrates, small lizards, nectar, juice from fruit

A NATIVE OF MADAGASCAR and nearby islands, the Madagascan Day Gecko has found a home in Florida, where it was released or escaped from the pet trade. As the name suggests, this species is out and about during the day. Its bright green color blends in well with the color of the leaves in its tropical home and in parts of Florida. These geckos may bite if they're disturbed.

RED LINE FROM SNOUT TO EYE

LARGE EYES SOMETIMES RINGED IN BLUE

RED SPOTS ON BACK

Mediterranean Gecko

Hemidactylus turcicus LENGTH 4–5 in (10–13 cm) ▪ HABITAT Tree bark, rock crevices, buildings ▪ RANGE Gulf Coast states; small colonies in other areas ▪ FOOD Insects

THIS NONNATIVE GECKO from the area around the Mediterranean Sea likes to be a housemate of humans. It's active at night, scurrying up walls and scampering along ceilings in pursuit of insects that gather near lights. Large toe pads help it climb well. It makes quiet, mouse-like squeaks as it hunts. Territorial males make chirping sounds when they approach females they're interested in.

ENLARGED TOE PADS

ROWS OF WHITE BUMPS EXTEND ONTO TAIL.

Green Anole

Anolis carolinensis LENGTH 5–8 in (13–20 cm) ▪ HABITAT Trees, shrubs, vines, walls, fence posts ▪ RANGE Southern Virginia to Florida to eastern Texas ▪ FOOD Insects, spiders, other invertebrates

THE GREEN ANOLE is the only anole native to the continental United States. Males have a pink dewlap, or throat fan. The fan enlarges during territory disputes or when there are females to impress. This species is active by day and can change color according to mood or environment. The Green Anole will head bob and do push-ups to accompany throat-fan extension and color change.

GREEN OR BROWN BODY

LONG, POINTED SNOUT

PINK THROAT FAN IN MALE

ENLARGED TOE PADS

Brown Anole

Anolis sagrei LENGTH 5–8 in (13–20 cm) ▪ HABITAT Close to ground in shrubs, trees, walls, rock piles ▪ RANGE Florida, southeastern Texas and nearby states ▪ FOOD Insects and spiders

BROWN ANOLES were introduced to the United States from the Caribbean Islands. When they change color, they stay in the gray to brown range, sometimes becoming darker. These anoles hang out closer to the ground than Green Anoles do. Brown Anole females don't have a dewlap, or throat fan, as males do. They do have a thin yellow stripe that sometimes runs down their back, flanked by half-moon shapes.

→ LISTEN FOR THIS
To tell the difference between a **BROWN ANOLE** and a **GREEN ANOLE**, it helps to know that the Green Anole can turn brown but the Brown Anole cannot turn green. Look also at the Brown's tail, which is flattened from side to side, and its reddish-orange—not pink—throat fan edged in white.

TAIL FLATTENED SIDE TO SIDE

SHORT SNOUT

REDDISH-ORANGE THROAT FAN WITH WHITE BORDER IN MALES

TAN TO BROWN TO GRAY COLOR

Eastern Collared Lizard

Crotaphytus collaris LENGTH 8–14 in (20–36 cm) ◦ HABITAT Rocky and hilly areas with shrubs, grasses, pine-juniper woodlands ◦ RANGE Southwestern Illinois to central Texas, west to Utah and Arizona ◦ FOOD Insects, spiders, other lizards, plants

THE MALE EASTERN COLLARED LIZARD is a cool creature. With his bright coloration and interesting pattern combination, he surely stands out. The female is a paler version of the male, and she lacks the bands found across the male's back. This species seems to like habitats with large boulders for basking in the sun and many rocky nooks and crannies for shelter and hiding places. An aggressive species, the Eastern Collared rushes at prey—often on its hind legs with its tail off the ground like a tiny tyrannosaur. When it gets close, it will quickly grab the prey.

10s spotters

BLACK AND WHITE COLLARS

GREEN BODY

SPOTTED TAIL

CROSSBANDS AND SPOTS ON BACK

→ **LOOK FOR THIS**
When a female **EASTERN COLLARED LIZARD** carries fertilized eggs inside her body, red or orange spots and bars appear along her sides outside her body. These fade after she lays her eggs. In midsummer, she lays up to a dozen eggs in a nest under a rock or in a rodent burrow that may still be occupied.

Laugh Out Loud!

Why did the lizard go on a diet?

If weighed too much for its scales!

REPTILE REPORT
Lizard Looks and Mighty Moves

LIZARDS ARE OFTEN very active and colorful creatures. Their coloring might blend in with the environment. Males of many species turn bright colors at breeding time to attract mates or warn off other males. Those with throat fans can flare them to look more impressive. They also strut their stuff by bobbing their heads and doing lizard push-ups. Not many female lizards change color at breeding time, but some develop color on their sides when they are carrying eggs. Lizards also have special adaptations that allow them to lose their tails easily if they're grabbed by a predator. This buys time for a speedy getaway. Some have specialized feet that allow them to travel on vertical surfaces—and even upside down! Check out more about these cool looks and moves.

A FEMALE COLLARED LIZARD BASKS
IN THE ARIZONA DESERT SUN.

Attractive!

This male anole displays his colorful, enlarged throat fan for the females he is trying to attract or the other males he is trying to keep away.

Tail Safety

Most lizards have built-in ways to ditch their tail when a predator comes after them. The tail separates from the body and continues to wiggle, while the rest of the lizard runs away. This confuses the predator. A lizard's tail usually breaks off neatly, and muscles keep the wound from bleeding too much. The tail grows back, but it will never look quite the same.

Fancy Feet

Gecko feet are amazing appendages. They allow the reptile to scurry up walls and run across ceilings, hanging on to grab insects attracted to lights. How do they do this? Tiny, hairlike structures called setae on the bottoms of gecko feet have what could be called a sticky and a nonsticky position. Gecko feet can switch between positions in an instant.

Long-nosed Leopard Lizard

Gambelia wislizenii LENGTH 8.5–15 in (22–38 cm) ◦ HABITAT Arid or semiarid areas with sand, gravel, low grasses, shrubs ◦ RANGE Southern Oregon and Idaho to New Mexico, west to California ◦ FOOD Insects, spiders, other lizards, snakes, rodents

IF YOU'RE A SMALL LIZARD living in the same area as a Long-nosed Leopard Lizard—watch out! The Long-nose has no problem eating other lizards. Like the closely related Eastern Collared Lizard, it often chases its prey on two legs. Females show orange spots and bars on their sides when they carry fertilized eggs, like female Eastern Collareds do. When the eggs are laid, the spots disappear.

GRAY TO BROWN BODY

ROUNDED TAIL

SPOTS FROM HEAD TO TAIL

Blunt-nosed Leopard Lizard

Gambelia sila LENGTH 3–5 in (8–13 cm) ◦ HABITAT Semiarid grasslands, washes, sandy and gravelly areas ◦ RANGE San Joaquin Valley, south-central California ◦ FOOD Insects, other lizards

THE BLUNT-NOSED LEOPARD LIZARD looks like the Long-nosed Lizard, but its nose is shorter and its head has a more triangular shape. It's a speedy species and is also able to jump almost two feet (0.6 m). This lizard is perfectly capable of digging its own burrow, but it often will use the burrows of rodents—sometimes when still occupied. Those burrows are usually deeper, which makes them good for brumation and for laying eggs.

save the lizards!

The Blunt-nosed Leopard Lizard's range has been greatly reduced by farming, ranching, and mining—and even by off-road vehicles, which harm their habitats. You can learn how they're being helped at californiaherps.com/lizards/pages/g.sila.html.

SMALL DARK SPOTS BETWEEN RINGS

BODY IS GRAY TO YELLOW.

LIGHT RINGS AROUND BODY

Jackson's Chameleon

Chamaeleo jacksonii LENGTH **6–12 in (15–30 cm)** ▫ HABITAT **Forests, orchards, wooded gardens** ▫ RANGE **Introduced into southern California** ▫ FOOD **Insects, spiders**

WHEN SOMEONE SAYS "LIZARD," many people think "chameleon," even though these colorful reptiles are not native to North America. The triple-horned Jackson's Chameleon, an East African native introduced into California, likes to live in trees, using its divided toes and prehensile tail to hold tight. To get water, it licks dew from leaves. The female Jackson's gives birth on tree branches to live young.

MALE HAS
3 HORNS.

FEMALE HAS
NO HORNS.

SMALL SPINES
ALONG BACK

BRIGHT GREEN COLOR

Oustalet's Chameleon

Furcifer oustaleti LENGTH **15–30 in (38–75 cm)** ▫ HABITAT **Many habitats, including farmland and housing developments** ▫ RANGE **Southern Florida** ▫ FOOD **Invertebrates, small birds, reptiles**

WHAT'S THE MEGA-SIZE OUSTALET'S CHAMELEON from Madagascar doing in southern Florida? It was introduced from the pet trade, then quickly adapted to life in the Sunshine State. Like other chameleons, it is a master prey-catcher, shooting out its tongue—longer than its body and with a sticky tip—in a fraction of a second. Eyes that rotate 180 degrees independently of each other is another chameleon advantage. The lizard can keep one eye on prey and the other on a predator.

RIDGES FROM
NOSE TO EYES

RIDGES FROM
EYE TO BACK
OF NECK

SPIKES ALONG
SPINE

BROWN, GREEN,
OR BLUE BODY

Desert Iguana

Dipsosaurus dorsalis LENGTH 10–16 in (25–40 cm) • HABITAT Arid brush and scrub with sand and rocks • RANGE Western Arizona to southeastern California • FOOD Leaves, buds, flowers of the creosote bush; other plants

BRING ON THE HEAT! The Desert Iguana tolerates heat better than many other desert animals, staying active even when temperatures soar. The range of this species is pretty much the same as the range of the arid-land creosote bush. It spends a lot of time munching on the parts of this bush and takes shelter in its shade. At night, Desert Iguanas bunk in rodent burrows, which they also use for a safe retreat when they feel threatened.

PALE HEAD

TAIL HAS BANDS OF DARK SPOTS.

NECK AND BODY HAVE A NETLIKE PATTERN WITH GRAY SPOTS.

10s spotters

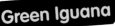

Green Iguana

Iguana iguana LENGTH 30–79 in (75–201 cm) • HABITAT Dense stands of trees, often near water • RANGE Southeastern Florida and several islands in the Florida Keys • FOOD Leaves, flowers, fruits

THIS NATIVE OF CENTRAL and South America was introduced into Florida because of the pet trade. The Green Iguana measures longer than the largest U.S. lizard, the Gila Monster. It also weighs a lot—up to 18 pounds (8 kg). At breeding time, males throw their weight around, fighting each other for mates. Successful males often are chosen as mates by multiple females.

→ LOOK FOR THIS
If you live or vacation in southeastern Florida, keep your eyes on the tops of trees. The **GREEN IGUANA** frequently hangs out in the canopies of trees that hang over water sources. If it feels unsafe, it will jump into the water, where it can stay submerged for up to half an hour.

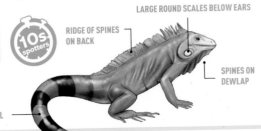

LARGE ROUND SCALES BELOW EARS

RIDGE OF SPINES ON BACK

SPINES ON DEWLAP

BANDS ON TAIL

10s spotters

Common Chuckwalla

Sauromalus ater LENGTH 11–16.5 in (28–42 cm) • HABITAT
Shrublands with rocky areas and lava flows • RANGE Western Arizona
to Southern California • FOOD Leaves, buds, flowers, insects

SMALL SCALES ON A BULKY BODY

make the Common Chuckwalla look even
bigger than its measurements suggest. But
this large lizard doesn't have a personality to
match its size. Instead, it tends to be timid.
When frightened, it often runs into a rock
crevice. Once inside, it gulps in air to inflate its
body until it's totally wedged in. A predator who
tries to pull it out will get frustrated pretty
fast. The chuckwalla is mostly an herbivore,
getting much of its nutrition from parts of the
creosote bush and other plants found in the
arid southwestern United States.

REPTILE file!

The name "chuckwalla" comes
from a Shoshone Indian word
that is often spelled *tcaxxwal*.
When Spanish settlers heard
the word, they spelled it
chacahuala. This eventually
became chuckwalla.

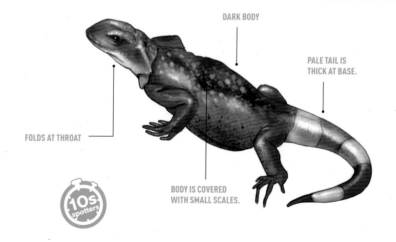

DARK BODY

PALE TAIL IS
THICK AT BASE.

FOLDS AT THROAT

BODY IS COVERED
WITH SMALL SCALES.

→ LOOK FOR THIS A young **COMMON CHUCKWALLA** starts out with dark bands across its body and tail. The
bands fade as it ages. In some areas of the chuckwalla's range, adult males have orange tails. Females usually keep
the dark bands throughout their lives.

Zebra-tailed Lizard

Callisaurus draconoides LENGTH 6–9 in (15–23 in) • HABITAT Dry areas with compact soil, rocks, little vegetation • RANGE Arizona, Nevada, Southern California • FOOD Insects, spiders, other lizards, plant matter

→ LOOK FOR THIS
The adult female **ZEBRA-TAILED** is one of the few female lizards that changes color when breeding. Since males and females both change color, you can tell the difference between a breeding male and a breeding female by the lack of stripes on the female's sides.

IF CHASED BY A FOX, snake, or other animal, the Zebra-tailed Lizard curls up its striped, tapering tail and waves it from side to side to distract the predator. Some researchers think a slim body and long legs help this quick-moving lizard—one of the fastest in the Southwestern desert lands—escape the animals that would like to make it a meal. Zebra-tails usually live in open areas. They are often active during the day, although they like to find their food in the morning before it gets too hot. The species digs its own burrows, which it uses for protection from predators and extreme temperatures.

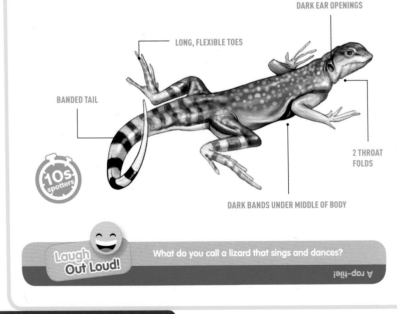

DARK EAR OPENINGS

LONG, FLEXIBLE TOES

BANDED TAIL

2 THROAT FOLDS

DARK BANDS UNDER MIDDLE OF BODY

10s spotters

Laugh Out Loud!

What do you call a lizard that sings and dances?

A rap-tile!

Common Lesser Earless Lizard

Holbrookia maculata LENGTH 4–5.5 in (10–14 cm) ▪ HABITAT Sand or gravel with short grass, pine-juniper woodlands, sagebrush, farmland ▪ RANGE Great Plains to northern Texas, Southwest region ▪ FOOD Insects, spiders, other lizards

EAR OPENINGS COULD BE A PROBLEM for a lizard that often burrows in sand, but the Common Lesser Earless Lizard doesn't have to worry—it doesn't have any, although it can hear. It has other adaptations that help it survive in its habitat, like small scales on its head and back and a valve that keeps sand out of its nose. Its color also helps it blend in with its environment. When in danger, this lizard may flee—or it can burrow its way out of trouble.

NO EAR OPENINGS

BELLY HAS 2 PAIRS OF BLACK MARKS.

TAN TO BROWN TO GRAY OR WHITE BODY

Greater Earless Lizard

Cophosaurus texanus LENGTH 3–7 in (8–18 cm) ▪ HABITAT Shrubland, rocky hillsides, sandy and gravelly areas ▪ RANGE Western Arizona, New Mexico, northern Texas ▪ FOOD Insects, spiders

THE GREATER EARLESS LIZARD can handle the heat. It does a better job of regulating its body temperature than some other hot-climate lizards. It places its body in different positions to get different amounts of sunlight, and it uses shade and burrowing to cool off. This allows it to be very active and have lots of time to forage for insects. Like the Zebra-tailed Lizard, this species runs from its enemies with its tail curled up and waving back and forth, displaying the black bars underneath.

NO EAR OPENINGS (EARS ARE INTERNAL.)

TAN

MALES HAVE 2 DARK BANDS ON BELLY AND SIDES.

FLAT BODY AND TAIL

BLACK CROSSBARS UNDER TAIL

Texas Horned Lizard

Phrynosoma cornutum LENGTH 2.5–7 in (6–18 cm) • HABITAT Arid areas with little grass or some shrubs • RANGE Kansas to Texas, west to Arizona • FOOD Ants, other insects, spiders

IN TEXAS, THE TEXAS HORNED LIZARD is a celebrity. As a college mascot, it goes by the name "Horned Frog." Many Texans also call it a horned toad. But this short, flat, squat reptile is all lizard. Color, pattern, and texture help camouflage the Texas Horned Lizard in its dry and dusty habitat. When feeling threatened, it shuffles sideways until it has dug itself into loose sand or soil. It also hides out in rock crevices, burrows of other animals—empty or not—and under bushes. This lizard often stations itself near an anthill and devours passing ants one by one.

True or False

Q: A Texas Horned Lizard never fights back when threatened.
A: False: It sometimes shoots a stream of blood from its eyelids.

Q: This lizard may gulp air to puff itself up to keep predators away.
A: True, and it sometimes pokes with its horns, or spines.

WHITE LINE ON BACK

2 ROWS OF POINTED SCALES ON SIDES

HORNS ON HEAD

BODY IS RED TO YELLOW TO GRAY.

10s spotters

REPTILE file!

In addition to camouflage, puffing up, and horn jabbing, the Texas Horned Lizard relies on another strategy when predators threaten it. It can shoot a stream of blood from openings in the corner of its eyes. The blood may travel several feet, and scientists think it probably tastes gross and scares the predator away.

Pygmy Short-horned Lizard

Phrynosoma douglasii LENGTH 2.5–5.5 in (6–14 cm) • HABITAT Plains, pine-juniper woodlands, mountains • RANGE Pacific Northwest, including Northern California • FOOD Ants, other insects

THE PYGMY SHORT-HORNED LIZARD

is a kind of a mini-version of a horned lizard. It has the toadlike body, head spines, and pointy side scales of other horned lizards, but all at a smaller size. This species lives a lot farther north and a lot higher up than most similar lizards—up to 6,000 feet (1,830 m). The Pygmy Short-horned also uses all the basic horned-lizard defensive tricks: hissing, biting, and shooting blood from the corners of its eyes. Scientists believe this lizard has disappeared from British Columbia, Canada, maybe due to climate change.

REPTILE file!

The Pygmy Short-horned Lizard's breeding season usually runs from July to September, but in some areas it may begin as early as May. Unusual among lizards, the female of this species bears live young. She will give birth to between 3 and 36 tiny lizards that look like mini-adults that measure less than an inch (25 mm) long.

BODY IS YELLOW TO GRAY TO REDDISH.

2 BARS ON EACH SIDE OF NECK

VERY SHORT HEAD SPINES

ONE ROW OF POINTED SCALES ON SIDES

10s spotters

Laugh Out Loud! How did the artist make her lizard sculpture?

She made a scale model.

Common Sagebrush Lizard

Sceloporus graciosus LENGTH 5–6.25 in (13–16 cm) • HABITAT Sagebrush, other brushlands, woodlands, mountain forests • RANGE Washington State to California, east to New Mexico, north to Montana • FOOD Insects, spiders

THE COMMON SAGEBRUSH LIZARD is a spiny lizard with keeled (ridged) and pointed scales on its back. It likes to hang out in the open as lizards do, soaking up rays on rocks or logs. But it's never more than a quick dash from the shelter of a rock crevice, an empty or occupied rodent burrow, or brush. These lizards may show yellow or orange on their neck and sides that's more noticeable in breeding females.

RUSTY PATCHES BEHIND FRONT LIMBS

BREEDING MALE HAS BLUE ON THROAT AND BELLY.

IRREGULAR STRIPES ON TOP

GRAY OR BROWN BODY

Desert Spiny Lizard

Sceloporus magister LENGTH 7–12 in (18–30 cm) • HABITAT Brush and scrublands in arid areas • RANGE Southern Nevada to California, east to Texas • FOOD Insects, spiders, other lizards, plants

THE DESERT SPINY LIZARD has tidy rows of keeled and pointed scales down its back—not a single scale seems out of place! Like many lizards, Desert Spinys darken in cool weather to absorb more heat, and they lighten up when it's warm. These lizards will become inactive in winter for a number of months that depends on the climate where they live. They often take shelter in Wood Rat nests that may still be occupied.

FEMALES HAVE ORANGE OR RED HEAD IN BREEDING SEASON.

SHOULDERS HAVE DARK TRIANGULAR PATCHES.

BROWNISH BODY

MALES MAY HAVE BLUE ON THROAT AND BELLY.

Western Fence Lizard

Sceloporus occidentalis LENGTH 6–9.25 in (15–23 cm) • HABITAT Grasslands, shrublands, woodlands, farmland • RANGE Washington State to California, Idaho to Utah • FOOD Insects, other small invertebrates

THE WESTERN FENCE LIZARD is pretty flexible when it comes to where it lives. It's found in many habitats, except extreme deserts. It likes to live in areas with rocks, woodpiles, and even old buildings. When the male wants to impress females, it flattens its body to show off the deep blue color on its lower sides. Like other male lizards, it also does push-ups and head-bobbing.

MALE HAS BLUE THROAT.

BLACK, GRAY, OR BROWN BODY

BLUE PATCHES ON BELLY

BLOTCHES OR CROSSBARS ON BODY

10s spotters

True or False

Q: The body of a Western Fence Lizard contains a protein that can knock out the Lyme disease bacterium.

A: True. When a tick that carries Lyme disease bites this lizard, the protein in the lizard's body clears the Lyme disease bacterium from the tick's body. Then it no longer carries the disease.

Eastern Fence Lizard

Sceloporus undulatus LENGTH 3.5–7.5 in (9–19 cm) • HABITAT Woodlands, grasslands, shrublands • RANGE New Jersey to Florida, west to Mississippi River • FOOD Insects, spiders, other invertebrates

THE EASTERN FENCE LIZARD has many different habits and routines that are determined by where it is living. In the eastern, wooded part of its range, it tends to climb trees. In the prairies, it spends a lot of time on the ground and in rodent burrows, sometimes with the rodents still living in another part. This species also is called the Pine Lizard because it has a habit of running up pine trees.

10s spotters

FEMALE HAS BARRED PATTERN ON BACK.

GRAY OR BROWN BODY

MALE HAS BLUE THROAT AND BELLY, BLUE-GREEN SIDES.

Ornate Tree Lizard

Urosaurus ornatus LENGTH 4.5–6.25 in (11–16 cm) ▪ HABITAT Arid areas with shrubs and trees, often along streams ▪ RANGE Southwestern Wyoming to western Texas, west to California ▪ FOOD Insects, other small invertebrates

NOW YOU SEE IT, NOW YOU DON'T. The color and pattern of an Ornate Tree Lizard blends well with tree bark and large boulders. When disturbed, this speedy and agile lizard retreats up a tree to stay out of view. It is out and about in the daytime searching for food. Even though they're territorial and spend a lot of time keeping others of their species out of their personal space, these lizards seek each other out to brumate in groups during the winter.

→ **LOOK FOR THIS**
This species is called **ORNATE**—which means fancily patterned—for the delicate lines on its head and for the other kinds of markings on its body, which can vary a lot.

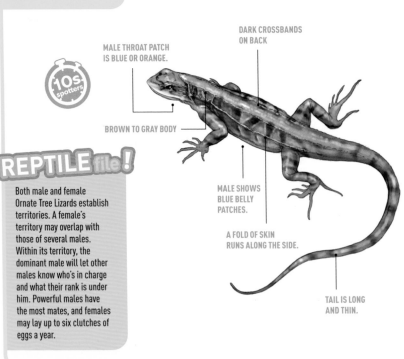

MALE THROAT PATCH IS BLUE OR ORANGE.

DARK CROSSBANDS ON BACK

BROWN TO GRAY BODY

MALE SHOWS BLUE BELLY PATCHES.

A FOLD OF SKIN RUNS ALONG THE SIDE.

TAIL IS LONG AND THIN.

10s spotters

REPTILE file!

Both male and female Ornate Tree Lizards establish territories. A female's territory may overlap with those of several males. Within its territory, the dominant male will let other males know who's in charge and what their rank is under him. Powerful males have the most mates, and females may lay up to six clutches of eggs a year.

Common Side-blotched Lizard

Uta stansburiana LENGTH 4–6.75 in (10–17 cm) • HABITAT
Grasslands, shrublands, other low-growing vegetation • RANGE Central
Washington State to Southern California to western Texas • FOOD
Insects, spiders, other small invertebrates

IF YOU'RE OUT LOOKING FOR LIZARDS
in the Southwest, there's a good chance
that you might meet up with the Common
Side-blotched Lizard. As the name suggests,
it's one of the most common around. These
lizards live on the ground and are active
during the day. They stay active year-round
in the southern parts of their range, where
the breeding season lasts longer and a female
lizard can lay up to seven clutches of one
to eight eggs a year. Northern Common
Side-blotcheds slow down in winter.

REPTILE file!

Some researchers think that
the color of a male Common
Side-blotched Lizard's throat
may determine how easily he
attracts a mate. Orange-
throated males attract a mate
more easily than blue-throated
ones. Blue-throats can keep
yellow-throats away from
the females simply because
they're more attractive than
the yellow-throats. But
yellow-throats, colored more
like females, can often trick
the orange-throats, then claim
the females for themselves.

COLOR AND BODY PATTERN VARY.

10s spotters

MALES SOMETIMES
SHOW BLUE COLOR
ON TAIL.

BLUE-BLACK SPOT
BEHIND FRONT LEGS

What powerful reptile can you find behind
closed curtains?

Laugh Out Loud!

The Lizard of Oz!

Southern Alligator Lizard

Elgaria multicarinata LENGTH 10–16 in (25–40 cm) • HABITAT Grasslands, open woods (especially oaks) • RANGE Southern Washington State to southwestern California • FOOD Insects, spiders, other invertebrates

REPTILE file!

Southern Alligator Lizards eat a wide range of invertebrates—even ones whose toxins, or poisons, affect other animals. These lizards often chow down on scorpions and Black Widow spiders.

ALLIGATOR LIZARDS ARE KNOWN for the folds on their sides made up of small scales. These folds allow the body to expand after a meal, because these lizards often eat prey as long as they are. The folds also allow females to make room for the 5 to 20 eggs they carry. Like alligators, alligator lizards have short legs that don't allow for speedy getaways. Instead they may wiggle, bite, and poop to defend themselves.

ARMORED SCALES ON HEAD, BODY, TAIL

REDDISH BROWN TO YELLOWISH GRAY BODY

DARK CROSSBANDS ON BACK AND TAIL

Texas Alligator Lizard

Gerrhonotus infernalis LENGTH 10–16 in (25–40 cm) • HABITAT Rocky hillsides, wooded canyons • RANGE West-central Texas • FOOD Insects, spiders, small snakes, other lizards, mammals

THE TEXAS ALLIGATOR LIZARD has armored scales on its head, body, and tail. Like alligators, these lizards have large, strong jaws that give them their common name. This species has a groove on the side of its body that allows the lizard to puff up and expand to make it look bigger and more threatening. This is a good strategy, because the Texas Alligator Lizard is a slow mover.

BODY IS YELLOW TO REDDISH BROWN.

SIDES HAVE LONG GROOVE.

BACK AND TAIL HAVE LIGHT CROSSBANDS.

Slender Glass Lizard

Ophisaurus attenuatus LENGTH 22–42 in (56–105 cm) •
HABITAT Dry grasslands, open woodlands • RANGE Virginia to Florida,
west to Texas, north to Wisconsin and Indiana • FOOD Insects, other
invertebrates, small mammals

WHAT'S LONG AND SLENDER and looks
like a snake, but isn't? If you said "Slender
Glass Lizard" or any of the other glass lizard
species, you'd be right. If you look closely, you
can tell it's not a snake from its movable eyelids
and ear openings. This limbless lizard has a
tail that breaks off pretty easily. It sometimes
breaks off when the lizard whips its body back
and forth. The tail will grow back in time. Few
of these lizards make it through life with their
original tail. Grooves on the side of the body,
like on some alligator lizards, allow expansion
and storage space for food and eggs.

REPTILE file!

Although side grooves give it
space to eat quite a bit, the
Slender Glass Lizard lacks
the flexible jaws snakes have
that allow them to get their
mouths around a mega meal.
This limits the size of prey
that glass lizards can eat.

DARK LINE DOWN
MIDDLE OF BACK

10S spotters

DARK LINES
BELOW GROOVE

LIGHT BROWN BODY

GROOVE ALONG SIDES

DON'T BE FOOLED Check out the **EASTERN GLASS LIZARD**
(*O. ventralis*), another member of the genus *Ophisaurus*, which means "snake lizard." It
resembles its close relative, the Slender Glass Lizard, but lacks the dark stripe down the
back and the dark lines below the side grooves. It also tends to turn greenish as it ages. Eastern Glass
Lizards live in the southeastern United States.

EXPERT'S CIRCLE

Gila Monster

Heloderma suspectum LENGTH 18–24 in (45–60 cm) • HABITAT Desert shrublands, oak woodlands • RANGE Southeastern California to New Mexico • FOOD Young birds, eggs, other lizards, insects, carrion

SMALL, BEADLIKE SCALES in unusual colors of peach, orange, yellow, and pink on a black background give the bulky, fat-tailed Gila (HEE-lah) Monster a unique look. It's unique in another way, too. It's the only venomous lizard in the United States. As the Gila Monster chomps on its victim, venom from glands in its jaws flows through grooves in its teeth. The venom may be mostly defensive, as a bite alone can take out only small prey, and the giant lizard's diet includes a lot of eggs and young birds. A Gila Monster can eat about a third of its weight in one meal. It spends most of its time in underground burrows.

REPTILE file!

Four or five hearty meals a year may be all the Gila Monster needs to survive. The slow and sleepy lizard doesn't need much energy. It spends a lot of its time resting underground and brumates in winter, surviving off the fat in its tail.

True or False

Q: The Gila Monster uses its forked tongue to sting its prey.
A: False. It uses its tongue to smell by gathering scent from the air.

Q: Male Gila Monsters wrestle each other to compete for mates.
A: True. They may wrestle for hours while the female watches.

Q: The Gila Monster can kill with its smelly breath.
A: False, but its breath does smell REALLY bad!

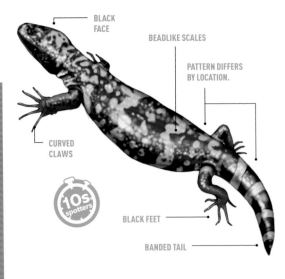

BLACK FACE

BEADLIKE SCALES

PATTERN DIFFERS BY LOCATION.

CURVED CLAWS

10s spotters

BLACK FEET

BANDED TAIL

Marbled Whiptail

Aspidoscelis marmorata LENGTH **8–12 in (20–30 cm)** •
HABITAT **Dry, sandy areas; woodland edges** • RANGE **Southern New
Mexico, western Texas** • FOOD **Insects**

A MARBLED WHIPTAIL does a jerky
side-to-side head snap when it's on
the prowl—just like the *Jurassic Park*
velociraptors. This is a feature of the whiptail
group of lizards, which have long, thin tails
like whips. Their bodies are also long and thin,
with small, bumpy scales called granules on
their backs and larger, squarish ones on their
undersides. Also like other whiptails, the marbled
species is pretty jumpy and will dash for cover
at the first sign of trouble. The Marbled Whiptail
has either a marbled pattern on its back or,
sometimes, a checkerboard-like pattern.

REPTILE file!

At breeding time, female
Marbled Whiptails lay one to
four eggs, often in May. The
eggs will hatch in July and
August. Hatchlings emerge
with bright blue tails, which
fade over time.

10s spotters

GRANULAR SCALES
ON BACK

MARBLED OR
CHECKERED
PATTERN ON
BACK

TAIL IS ABOUT 3
TIMES BODY LENGTH.

BELLY HAS 8 ROWS OF
RECTANGULAR SCALES.

Why was the lizard in Hufflepuff?

Because he wasn't Slytherin'!

Laugh Out Loud!

Six-lined Racerunner

Aspidoscelis sexlineata LENGTH 6–9.5 in (15–24 cm) • HABITAT Grasslands, open woodlands, other open ground • RANGE Southeastern and south-central U.S. • FOOD Insects

THE ONLY KIND OF WHIPTAIL LIZARD that can be found in the eastern United States is the Six-lined Racerunner. This lizard relies on its awesome speed to get out of danger. Racerunners are active during the day, especially in the morning. They dart here and there over open areas looking for a meal—large grasshoppers are a favorite. Because people rarely catch more than a glimpse of this speedy lizard, another common name is Fieldstreak. Trying to chase one would probably end with the racerunner disappearing into vegetation, rocks, or burrows, which the lizards sometimes dig themselves. These speedy, streamlined lizards have been clocked at 18 miles per hour (29 km/h).

→ **LOOK FOR THIS**
You'll have to look sharp—and fast—for the six or seven light stripes across the **SIX-LINED RACERUNNER'S** back and sides. This species can be mistaken for some local skink species that have six stripes on the back and sides—but they're not the real thing!

10s spotters

BODY HAS 6 OR 7 LIGHT STRIPES BORDERED BY DARK BANDS.

MALE HAS GREEN OR BLUE THROAT.

FEMALE HAS WHITE THROAT.

REPTILE file!

Female Six-lined Racerunners lay five to six eggs in shallow soil, or even in sawdust piles. Older females at the peak of their breeding abilities tend to lay bigger eggs and often lay two clutches of eggs in a year.

Tiger Whiptail

Aspidoscelis tigris LENGTH **8–12 in (20–30 cm)** • HABITAT **Desert; dry, open woodlands** • RANGE **Eastern Oregon and western Idaho to Southern California and western Texas** • FOOD **Insects, scorpions, other small invertebrates**

LIKE OTHER LIZARDS in the whiptail group, the Tiger Whiptail has a long thin tail that helps it balance while running. Also known as the Western Whiptail, this species shows different patterns of spots and bars on its back as well as long, light stripes along its body. As these lizards age, though, the stripes fade and the patterns may grow together into larger blotches.

POINTY NOSE

DARK SPOTS AND BARS ON BACK

FAINT STRIPES

Plateau Striped Whiptail

Aspidoscelis velox LENGTH **8–10.75 in (20–27 cm)** • HABITAT **Pine-juniper and oak woodlands, pine and fir forests, chaparral** • RANGE **Western Colorado and New Mexico to northeastern Arizona and southeastern Utah** • FOOD **Insects, other small invertebrates**

Believe it or not, all Plateau Striped Whiptails are female. How can this be? This species has the ability to lay unfertilized—yet fertile— eggs that hatch into only female lizards. The babies are basically clones of the mother. Plateau Stripeds are a bit less nervous when disturbed than other whiptails. They may run away, but they don't go as far away.

7 LIGHT STRIPES ON BACK

TAIL IS PALE BLUE.

BLUISH ON CHIN AND UNDERSIDE

Common Five-lined Skink

Plestiodon fasciatus LENGTH 5–8.5 in (13–22 cm) • HABITAT Humid woodlands with debris cover, gardens • RANGE Southern New England to Florida, west to Texas, north to Great Lakes • FOOD Insects, other invertebrates, other lizards, mice

GLOSSY BODY IS BROWN TO BLACK.

BODY HAS 5 CREAM TO WHITE STRIPES.

LONG TAIL IS BLUE TO GRAY.

WHEN IN DANGER FROM A PREDATOR, skinks let go of their tails (see page 45). They make use of this common lizard feature very frequently. The Common Five-lined Skink prefers habitats with leaf litter and decaying wood that contain lots of insects. They also use rock ledges for shelter. Females lay their 5 to 15 eggs in fallen logs and other places that offer some protection. They will turn the eggs daily. Once the eggs hatch, the babies are on their own.

Broad-headed Skink

Plestiodon laticeps LENGTH 5.5–12.75 in (14–32 cm) • HABITAT Woodlands and open areas with leaf litter and other debris • RANGE Southeastern Pennsylvania to Florida, west to Kansas and Texas • FOOD Insects, other invertebrates, fruit

FOR A SKINK, the male Broad-headed Skink has a large head that really stands out during breeding season, when it turns reddish orange. This feature gave the species the nickname "red-headed scorpion." The Broad-headed Skink is active during the day and often is found in trees, searching for insects and their larvae to eat. Males fight each other for mates. Females seem to go for males with the brightest orange heads.

REPTILE file!

The female Broad-headed Skink often lays her clutch of 6 to 16 eggs in holes in trees. She takes care of the eggs—as skinks typically do—circling the nest with her body and turning the eggs every day until they hatch in two to three months.

BLUE TO BROWN TAIL

BROWN BODY WITH 5 LIGHT STRIPES THAT FADE IN ADULT MALES

BROAD HEAD

Western Skink

Plestiodon skiltonianus LENGTH 6.5–9.25 in (16.5–23 cm) ▪ HABITAT
Grasslands, shrublands, forests, open woods ▪ RANGE British Columbia to California
and northern Arizona ▪ FOOD Insects, spiders, other invertebrates

LIKE OTHER SKINKS, a breeding male Western
Skink is reddish orange around the mouth and
chin, but it doesn't stop there. It often displays
reddish coloring on its sides and on the tip
and underside of its tail. The young Western
Skink is also hard to miss because of its bright
colors, wide brown stripe down its back, and
bright blue tail. When in danger, this skink easily
leaves its tail behind to distract and
confuse predators.

→ LOOK FOR THIS
WESTERN SKINKS are hard to
find. They're active during the day
but are very shy and secretive. They
often hide under rocks and woody
debris. If disturbed, they take off
like a rocket, with only the flash
of their blue tail.

FOUR LIGHT
LINES ON BODY

SHINY BODY

BROWN CENTRAL
LINE DOWN BACK

BLUE OR GRAY TAIL

10s
spotters

Florida Sand Skink

Plestiodon reynoldsi LENGTH 4–5 in (10–13 cm) ▪ HABITAT Scrublands,
dry uplands ▪ RANGE Central Florida ▪ FOOD Beetle larvae, termites, other insects
and larvae

IF YOU DON'T GET A GOOD LOOK at a Florida
Sand Skink, you might think you've seen a snake.
This skink has legs, but they are small and almost
useless. It's not a huge problem, though, because
the sand skink spends a lot of time below the
surface of the sand "swimming" in search of the
insects and larvae it likes to eat. Young Florida
Sand Skinks tend to have a wide line that extends
from nose to tail on each side.

10s
spotters

GRAY, WHITE,
OR TAN BODY

TINY LEGS

NO EXTERNAL
EARS

WEDGE-SHAPED SNOUT

Little Brown Skink

Scincella lateralis LENGTH 3–5.5 in (8–14 cm) ▪ HABITAT Moist forests, forested grasslands, gardens ▪ RANGE New Jersey to Florida, west to Texas and Nebraska ▪ FOOD Insects, spiders, other invertebrates

SMALL AND AGILE, the Little Brown Skink wiggles from side to side as it runs. At the small end of its size range, this species measures only three inches (8 cm) long—and that includes the tail! Also known as the Ground Skink, the Little Brown Skink has a transparent disk in each eyelid that acts like a window and allows the skink to see when its eyes are closed. This adaptation helps it see where it's going in deep leaf litter, which makes it easy to find the insects and spiders it loves to eat while remaining safe from predators. Unlike skinks in the genus *Plestiodon*, the female Little Brown Skink does not take care of her eggs in the nest.

→ **LISTEN FOR THIS**
Usually the smallest lizards in their range, **LITTLE BROWN SKINKS** can be hard to spot. It's often easier to hear them. If you're in the woods and hear a rustling in the leaves on the ground, it might be a skink on a mission—to get from point A to point B and maybe grab some tasty spiders along the way!

SHINY BROWN OR GOLDEN TAN BODY

DARK LINE ON SIDES

JUVENILE SKINKS HAVE BLUE TAILS.

10s spotters

Florida Wormlizard

Rhineura floridana LENGTH **7–11 in (18–28 cm)** • HABITAT **Dry, sandy soil** • RANGE **Northern and central Florida, very limited in Georgia** • FOOD **Earthworms, termites, spiders**

LOOKING LIKE A GIANT, often pinkish earthworm, the Florida Wormlizard is the only North American representative of a reptile group once known as amphisbaenians. Mostly legless, wormlizards look like snakes, but they're really lizards. The Florida Wormlizard has features that allow it to live underground. A wedge-shaped head that lacks external eyes and ears lets it burrow easily into sandy soil, aided by a short and somewhat tapered tail. Heavy rains sometimes flush the wormlizard out of the soil. This can fool birds hoping to snag a big, fat earthworm—they might get a nasty wormlizard bite instead.

→ **LOOK FOR THIS**
FLORIDA WORMLIZARDS live most of their lives underground in areas of sandhills and oak forests. They don't stray too far from the surface of the ground and sometimes can be found just under leaf litter. They also turn up in plowed fields and turned-over soil in gardens.

10s. spotters

REPTILE file!

Because of their secretive, underground lives, not much is known about wormlizard reproduction. Scientists do know that females lay one to three long, oval eggs underground in the summer that hatch in the fall.

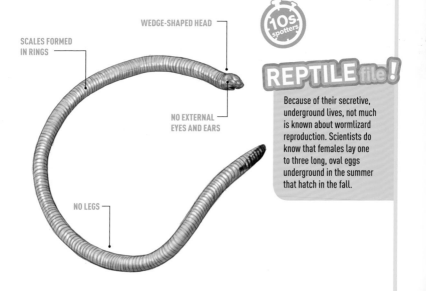

WEDGE-SHAPED HEAD

SCALES FORMED IN RINGS

NO EXTERNAL EYES AND EARS

NO LEGS

SNAKES

Western Threadsnake

Rena humilis LENGTH **7–16 in (18–40 cm)** ▪ HABITAT **Deserts, grasslands, canyons** ▪ RANGE **Southern Utah, Nevada, California to southern Arizona, New Mexico, and western Texas** ▪ FOOD **Termites, ants**

THE WESTERN THREADSNAKE has black dots on the sides of its head. These are sightless eyes that are covered by scales. This species belongs to a group of burrowing snakes that are blind. These reptiles are difficult to spot. They live underground or beneath rocks, coming out after heavy rains or to search for termites and ants to eat.

BROWN, PINK, OR PURPLISH BODY

SMOOTH, SHINY SCALES

ONE SCALE BETWEEN EYES

SPINE ON TIP OF TAIL

10s spotters

Texas Threadsnake

Rena dulcis LENGTH **5–11.5 in (13–29 cm)** ▪ HABITAT **Prairies, canyons, deserts** ▪ RANGE **Southern Kansas to Texas, west to southern Arizona** ▪ FOOD **Termites, ants**

THE TEXAS THREADSNAKE lives in the same kinds of habitats as its relative, the Western Threadsnake. It also eats the same kinds of food. These snakes are out and about above ground after spring and summer rains, and often at night. They find ant nests to raid by following the scent trails of ants along the ground. They eat ants of any age, from egg to adult.

MORE THAN ONE SCALE BETWEEN EYES

10s spotters

SPINE ON TIP OF TAIL

BROWN, PINK, OR REDDISH BODY

REPTILE file!

After mating, the female Texas Threadsnake lays a clutch of two to seven very slender, almost needlelike eggs. These snakes often come together to lay their eggs in a communal nest. They guard their eggs by coiling around them until they are ready to hatch.

Northern Rubber Boa

Charina bottae LENGTH 14–33 in (36–84 cm) ▪ HABITAT Damp woodlands, coniferous forests, chaparral, grasslands ▪ RANGE British Columbia, Canada, to Southern California, east to Utah, Wyoming, and Montana ▪ FOOD Small mammals, birds, lizards, salamanders

THE NORTHERN RUBBER BOA doesn't have the word "rubber" in its name for nothing. It looks a lot like a toy rubber snake. Boas, like pythons, kill their prey by coiling their bodies around the victim and squeezing it, making it suffocate. When threatened, a Northern Rubber Boa often forms a tight ball with its body, with the blunt tail sticking out, possibly so it looks like the head, which is tucked down safely into the coils. This snake can live more than 40 years and is a champion burrower, climber, and swimmer. Females give birth to two to eight live young.

→ **LOOK FOR THIS**
If you look on the underside of the **NORTHERN RUBBER BOA,** you'll see small spurs behind the vent (the opening used for excretion and reproduction). They are the remnants of legs that snakes used to have when they were evolving from lizards more than 100 million years ago.

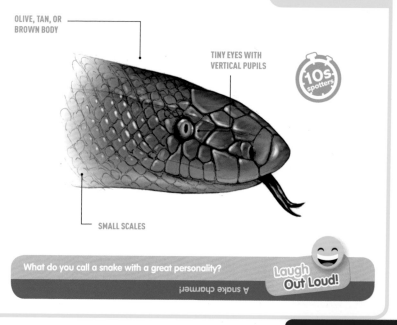

OLIVE, TAN, OR BROWN BODY

TINY EYES WITH VERTICAL PUPILS

10s spotters

SMALL SCALES

What do you call a snake with a great personality?

A snake charmer!

Laugh Out Loud!

Boa Constrictor

Boa constrictor LENGTH 5–7 ft (1.5–2 m) • HABITAT Pine rocklands, hardwood hammocks, limestone walls, along canals • RANGE Miami area of southern Florida • FOOD Mammals, birds, lizards, fish

BOA CONSTRICTORS were brought into the United States as pets from Central and South America. They are now an invasive species that threatens native wildlife in southern Florida—and they could easily move into other areas. These strong snakes grasp their prey with a jaw full of small, curved teeth and then coil their body around it. They squeeze tightly with their strong muscles to kill the victim. If disturbed, Boa Constrictors may strike quickly. They are not venomous, but they can deliver a painful bite.

REPTILE file!

A female Boa Constrictor incubates 20 to 30 eggs inside her body. When it's time to give birth, she delivers live young that can be more than a foot (30 cm) in length. Like all snakes, the young are ready to take care of themselves at birth.

TAN TO LIGHT BROWN BODY

DARK BROWN SADDLE PATTERN ON BACK

10s spotters

TRIANGLE PATTERN TOWARD TAIL

True or False

Q: Boa Constrictors are one of only a few animal species with a common name that's the same as the scientific name.
A: True.

Q: A group of boas is called a wriggle.
A: False. A group of boas is called a bed or knot.

North American Racer

Coluber constrictor **LENGTH** 3–5 ft (0.9–1.5 m) • **HABITAT** Fields, grasslands, brush, open woodlands, rocky hillsides • **RANGE** Much of central and eastern U.S., southernmost Ontario, Canada • **FOOD** Insects, lizards, snakes, birds, small rodents

NORTH AMERICAN RACERS don't waste any time when they travel from one place to another. They skim along the ground with their head held high, almost like a hovercraft. You may get only a quick glimpse of one in the grass or crossing a road. When a racer snake feels threatened, it may vibrate its tail in dry leaves to create a rattling sound that may scare off a predator.

→ LOOK FOR THIS
Although the **NORTHERN RACER'S** scientific name includes the word "constrictor," it does not constrict and squeeze its prey. Instead, it pins the victim down using a loop of its long, slender body and then swallows it whole.

BODY IS BLACK, BROWN, BLUE, OR GREEN ABOVE.

WHITE, YELLOW, OR GRAY UNDERNEATH

SLENDER, POINTED TAIL

Coachwhip

Coluber flagellum **LENGTH** 3.5–5 feet (1–1.5 m) • **HABITAT** Grasslands, pastures, scrublands, open woodlands • **RANGE** Southern half of U.S. • **FOOD** Frogs, lizards, snakes, baby turtles, birds

THE COACHWHIP gets its name from a long tail with scales that make it look like a braided whip. People once believed that after this species captured its prey, it used its tail to whip it to death. In reality, it pounces on its prey and bites it, tearing the skin. One of North America's fastest snakes, it keeps its head up as it travels to locate a meal.

LONG, THIN TAIL

BODY IS TAN, BROWN, YELLOW, OR EVEN RED IN WEST.

BODY IS LIGHTER TOWARD THE REAR IN EAST.

HEAD IS DARK BROWN TO BLACK IN EAST.

Texas Indigo Snake

Drymarchon melanurus erebennus LENGTH 5–6.5 ft (1.5–2 m) ○ HABITAT Grasslands, shrublands, sand dunes, near water ○ RANGE Southern third of Texas ○ FOOD Small mammals, turtles, frogs, snakes

THE THICK-BODIED, very long, and shiny blue-black Texas Indigo Snake is out and about during the day. On the hunt early in the morning, it feeds its impressive appetite with a diet of mammals, turtles, frogs, and other snakes—including cottonmouths and rattlesnakes. The nonvenomous indigo snake grasps a venomous snake by the head and bashes and chews until it is able to swallow the rest of its meal. The venom stored in the victim's head seems not to harm the indigo snake. Scientists think the snakes have developed an immunity to it. Texas Indigo Snakes like to sun themselves along river and canal banks or hang out coiled up in the low branches of trees. They can remain active in mild winter weather, when they breed.

→ LOOK FOR THIS
When threatened, a **TEXAS INDIGO SNAKE** acts like a venomous snake. It flattens its neck, hisses, and vibrates its tail to get attackers to take it seriously.

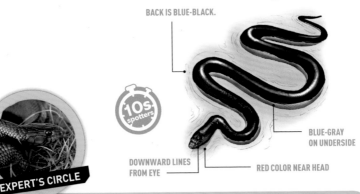

BACK IS BLUE-BLACK.

10s spotters

DOWNWARD LINES FROM EYE

RED COLOR NEAR HEAD

BLUE-GRAY ON UNDERSIDE

EXPERT'S CIRCLE

DON'T BE FOOLED The related **EASTERN INDIGO SNAKE** *(Drymarchon couperi)* is the longest native snake species in the United States, measuring up to 8.6 feet (2.6 m). It lives in the southeastern United States and has the typical shiny blue-black indigo snake look, but it is set apart from the Texas Indigo Snake by some cream or red on the chin and throat.

California Kingsnake

Lampropeltis californiae LENGTH 30–41 in (75–105 cm) • HABITAT Chaparral, grasslands, woodlands, marshes • RANGE Southern Oregon to Southern California, east to western Arizona • FOOD Small mammals, lizards, snakes, amphibians, birds, eggs

THE NONVENOMOUS CALIFORNIA KINGSNAKE defends itself with some of the behaviors used by indigo snakes and other members of the colubrid family of snakes. It hisses and rattles its tail when threatened. In predator mode, it kills its prey with powerful constrictions and also eats venomous snakes. The kingsnake is immune to its victims' venom.

REPTILE file!

The female California Kingsnake lays about two dozen eggs in places such as rotting logs. The eggs hatch in about two months, and the baby snakes measure about a foot (30 cm) long.

BLACK OR BROWN BODY

MOSTLY WHITE FACE

WHITE OR YELLOW CROSSBANDS ON BACK

Yellow-bellied Kingsnake

Lampropeltis calligaster LENGTH 30–41 in (75–105 cm) • HABITAT Grasslands, open woodlands, savanna • RANGE Maryland to northern Florida, west to Nebraska and Texas • FOOD Rodents, birds, lizards, frogs, snakes

IF YOU WANT TO SEE a Yellow-bellied Kingsnake, look for one after it rains. Storms often bring this secretive species out into the open, where it can be seen crossing roads. Otherwise, it is well camouflaged among vegetation by its markings, which may become less distinct with age. The Yellow-bellied Kingsnake spends a lot of time burrowing in loose soil or under rocks.

→ **LOOK FOR THIS**
The color and pattern of a **YELLOW-BELLIED KINGSNAKE** make it easy to mistake for a copperhead—which is venomous.

BROWN MARKINGS EDGED IN BLACK ON BACK

BELLY IS BLOTCHY YELLOW.

SMALLER SIDE MARKINGS

Eastern Kingsnake

Lampropeltis getula LENGTH 36–47 in (90–120 cm) • HABITAT Pine woods, swamps, marshes, stream banks, old buildings • RANGE New Jersey to northern Florida, west to Appalachians, southern Alabama • FOOD Rodents, lizards, snakes, birds, eggs

THE EASTERN KINGSNAKE has a pattern of white crossbands with irregular edges that make it look like a chain is wrapped around its body. It's no surprise that another name for this constrictor is Chain Kingsnake. This smooth and shiny snake is often active during the day. In hot weather, it changes its routine, becoming active at night and spending the day underground to stay cool.

WHITE, CREAM, OR YELLOW CROSSBANDS

BLACK OR DARK BROWN BODY

WHITE OR YELLOW SPLOTCHES ON BELLY

Western Milksnake

Lampropeltis gentilis LENGTH 24–35 in (60–90 cm) • HABITAT Prairies, rocky areas • RANGE Louisiana west of Mississippi River, west to Arizona, north to South Dakota and Montana • FOOD Rodents, birds, lizards, snakes

MILKSNAKES get their name from the old superstition that the snake "milks" cows, robbing them of their milk. There are different varieties of milksnakes, with different colors and patterns. Some resemble copperheads and coralsnakes. In milksnakes, a black ring separates red and yellow rings. In the venomous coralsnakes, the red and yellow rings are next to each other. The milksnake has the red and yellow "caution colors" of the coralsnake (see page 97) to give predators the impression that it could be dangerous.

RED, ORANGE, OR BLACK COLOR EXTENDS ONTO THE BELLY.

HEAD BLACK, SNOUT USUALLY WHITE

RED/ORANGE, BLACK, AND YELLOW/WHITE RINGS

Smooth Greensnake

Opheodrys vernalis LENGTH 12–20 in (30–50 cm) ▪ HABITAT Meadows, fields, fencerows, grassy marshes ▪ RANGE Extreme southern and eastern Canada, north-central and northeastern U.S. ▪ FOOD Insects, spiders

THIS IS ONE SMOOTH SNAKE, with a shiny, slender body and an even more slender tail. Nonvenomous and harmless, the Smooth Greensnake may gape—showing a wide-open mouth—if grabbed, but it seldom bites. It enjoys a social life, too, often spending the winter in a large group to stay warm. Females also may share a communal site where they lay their eggs. When a Smooth Greensnake dies, it immediately turns dull blue.

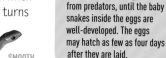

REPTILE file!

The female Smooth Green Snake can lay her eggs several months after breeding. She keeps them warm inside her body, safe from predators, until the baby snakes inside the eggs are well-developed. The eggs may hatch as few as four days after they are laid.

SMOOTH, GRASS-GREEN BODY

SLENDER, TAPERING TAIL

WHITE TO YELLOW UNDERNEATH

Rough Greensnake

Opheodrys aestivus LENGTH 22–32 in (56–81 cm) ▪ HABITAT Open forests, shrubs, near wetlands and rivers ▪ RANGE Southern New Jersey to Florida, west to Texas ▪ FOOD Insects, spiders

AT FIRST GLANCE, the Rough Greensnake looks similar to the smooth species, but look closely, and you'll see that its scales have keels, or ridges, and it is longer. It also likes to climb more than the Smooth Greensnake does, earning it the nickname "vine snake." When a Rough Greensnake searches for prey, it lifts its head up like a telescope above the vegetation to get a good look.

LARGE EYES

WHITE OR YELLOW UNDERNEATH

BRIGHT GREEN BODY

Eastern Ratsnake

Pantherophis alleghaniensis LENGTH 3.5–6 ft (1–1.8 m) ▪ HABITAT
Hardwood forests, thickets, swamps, fields, barnyards, backyards ▪ RANGE From Florida
as far north as eastern New York ▪ FOOD Birds, eggs, salamanders, lizards, rodents

→ LOOK FOR THIS
Not all **EASTERN RATSNAKES**
look the same. Some keep the
dark splotches that juveniles
usually have on their gray bodies.
In Florida, snakes have a tan to
yellow body with four long stripes.

FORMERLY KNOWN AS THE BLACK RATSNAKE,
this species has a squarish body that has been
compared in shape to a loaf of bread. It is a
powerful constrictor, often hiding along the
beaten paths that small rodents use, ready to
attack. The Eastern Ratsnake climbs with ease
and may drape itself on a branch above a trail,
surprising hikers. This snake often brumates
in groups that include other species, including
venomous copperheads.

10s spotters

CHECKERBOARD
PATTERN ON THE BELLY

TYPICALLY BLACK ABOVE

WHITE UNDER CHIN

Red Cornsnake

Pantherophis guttatus LENGTH 30–47 in (75–120 cm) ▪ HABITAT Woodlands,
meadows, prairies, barnyards, abandoned buildings ▪ RANGE Southern New Jersey
to Florida, west to Louisiana ▪ FOOD Rodents, birds, lizards

A CLOSE RELATIVE OF the Eastern Ratsnake,
the Red Cornsnake is considered one of the
most colorful reptiles in the East. But this
species is more shy than its cousin, preferring
to spend a lot of time underground in rodent
burrows. The Red Cornsnake regularly prowls
storage buildings that hold harvested grain and
hay in search of rodents that nibble grain and
seeds. When threatened, it may rise from its
coils to appear bigger.

BODY IS ORANGE,
BROWNISH, OR GRAYISH.

10s spotters

CHECKERBOARD
PATTERN ON UNDERSIDE

BLACK-EDGED REDDISH,
BROWN, OR GRAY BLOTCHES

Pinesnake

Pituophis melanoleucus LENGTH 4–5.6 ft (1.2–1.7 m) • HABITAT
Pine and pine-oak woods, sandy areas, fields • RANGE Mid-Atlantic and
southeastern U.S. • FOOD Mainly rodents

THE PINESNAKE'S KEELED (ridged)
scales look a lot like grains of barley,
especially in snakes with a tan or brown
body. This large constrictor will look different
depending on location. The mid-Atlantic
Pinesnake is usually white with black blotches.
Florida snakes are gray to brown, with muddled
blotches. Those in Louisiana have brownish
blotches near the head and sharper reddish
ones near the tail. When disturbed, the
Pinesnake makes a big fuss. It hisses loudly,
vibrates its tail, and flattens its head like a
cobra. All this makes it seem like a scarier,
venomous snake—but it's not!

REPTILE file!

The female Pinesnake digs a
side chamber in her burrow as
a nest, where she will lay 3 to
24 eggs. A number of different
females may use the chamber
year after year.

PATTERN VARIES.

LARGE SCALE
ON NOSE

10s spotters

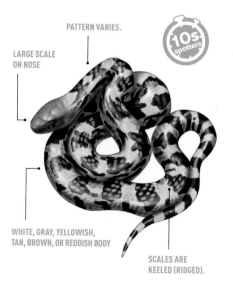

WHITE, GRAY, YELLOWISH,
TAN, BROWN, OR REDDISH BODY

SCALES ARE
KEELED (RIDGED).

MAKE THIS!

Dig up some fun
facts and fascinating
information and make a
snake info poster!

1. Include pictures that
   show the differences
   between venomous
   and nonvenomous
   snakes. (See page 88.)
2. Present facts about
   snake behavior.
3. List reasons why
   people should protect
   snakes and how to
   do it.
4. Share your poster with
   family and friends.

REPTILE REPORT
Snakes on the Move

MOVING FROM ONE PLACE to another is called locomotion, and snakes move (or locomote) in mysterious ways. Without legs, they have to push themselves forward or sideways, whether it's across the ground or up a tree. During their locomotion, snakes leave cool tracks in their path. As you walk in soil or sand, look for tracks that may tell you that a snake has wandered through ahead of you. There are four basic moves that snakes make. Check them out here.

Classic Move

The "classic" snake motion used by most snakes is the serpentine method (from the word "serpent," of course). It's also known as lateral undulation. In this move, a snake pushes off tiny bumps on the surface to get a wavy motion going. This method doesn't work very well on slick surfaces, though, where there are no bumps to help the snake gain traction.

A SIDEWINDER RATTLESNAKE MAKES ITS SIGNATURE PATH THROUGH DESERT DUNES IN NEW MEXICO, U.S.A.

Play That Accordion!

The concertina motion is named for the concertina instrument, which is a relative of the accordion. During this movement, a snake braces its back end in folds to gain friction and then pushes the straightened front end forward. As the front arrives, the snake folds its back end again to gain friction. The movement is repeated. Species such as kingsnakes use this method to climb trees or travel through narrow spaces.

Straight Arrow

In the rectilinear, or straight, method, a snake creeps along in a straight line using its muscles to make its belly scales grip the surface. As the snake scales stretch, the muscles lift the snake and push it forward. Large-bodied snakes like boas and pythons use this method.

Going Sideways

In sidewinding, a snake moves by placing part of its body against the ground, then lifting portions of the body off the ground. This propels the snake sideways and slightly forward, leaving J-shaped tracks in sand. Desert-dwelling snakes like Sidewinders sidewind to avoid too much body contact with hot sand and to climb steep sand dunes.

Southeastern Crowned Snake

Tantilla coronata LENGTH 8–10 in (20–25 cm) ◦ HABITAT Pine woods, oak-hickory forests, scrublands, grasslands ◦ RANGE Southeastern U.S., only Panhandle in Florida ◦ FOOD Earthworms, slugs, insect larvae

THE SOUTHEASTERN CROWNED SNAKE has a black head and chin, as well as a light band that looks like a collar at the base of its head. This small and otherwise plain snake often goes unnoticed, even though it appears in urban backyards. It often stays hidden under rotten logs, leaf litter, and piles of debris, its color blending with the soil. It feasts on earthworms and other ground-dwelling prey.

LIGHT COLLAR

TAN OR REDDISH TAN BODY

BLACK CAP, CHIN, AND NECK BLOTCH

WHITISH UNDERSIDE

Long-nosed Snake

Rhinocheilus lecontei LENGTH 20–60 in (50–150 cm) ◦ HABITAT Scrublands, grasslands, chaparral ◦ RANGE Southwestern U.S. to Northern California, Idaho, Colorado ◦ FOOD Lizards, lizard eggs, small mammals, birds

WHEN DISTURBED, the Long-nosed Snake makes a big stink about it by twisting its body, vibrating its tail, and excreting poop and blood. Gross, but it works! The Long-nose spends most of its day underground. It's active at dawn and dusk and during the night, when it hunts lizards and other preferred prey. On warm summer evenings, it often can be seen crossing roads in desert areas.

REPTILE file!

Female Long-nosed Snakes lay four to nine eggs underground in early summer. The eggs hatch 40 to 90 days later, in the fall.

JAW IS INSET.

REDDISH OR PINK BETWEEN SADDLES

BACK HAS BLACK SADDLES EDGED IN WHITE.

LONG, POINTY SNOUT

SINGLE ROW OF ENLARGED SCALES UNDER TAIL

Common Wormsnake

Carphophis amoenus LENGTH 7.5–11 in (19–28 cm) ▪ HABITAT Fields, meadows, woodlands, vacant lots ▪ RANGE Southern New England to Georgia, west to Mississippi River ▪ FOOD Earthworms, soft-bodied insects

THE COMMON WORMSNAKE looks like—you guessed it!—a worm. But it also counts worms among its favorite food groups. And animals that eat worms, such as birds and other snakes, also eat the wormsnake. This shy snake prefers a moist habitat and seeks out hiding places beneath rocks, rotting logs, boards, and leaf litter. It spends a lot of time underground, using its pointed head and thin, smooth body and tapered tail to burrow into the soil. This helps it stay warm in cool or dry weather. Because it burrows, it often turns up as worms do when the soil is turned over for gardening or when a field is plowed.

REPTILE file!

Common Wormsnakes have both a spring and fall mating season. Females lay one to eight eggs underground that hatch in about seven weeks. Baby wormsnakes, about four inches (10 cm) long, look even more like worms than their parents!

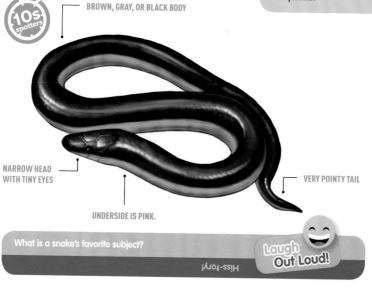

10s spotters

BROWN, GRAY, OR BLACK BODY

NARROW HEAD WITH TINY EYES

UNDERSIDE IS PINK.

VERY POINTY TAIL

What is a snake's favorite subject?

Hiss-tory!

Laugh Out Loud!

Ring-necked Snake

Diadophis punctatus LENGTH 10–30 in (25–75 cm) ◦ HABITAT Woodlands, grasslands, hillsides, upland deserts ◦ RANGE Nova Scotia, Canada, to Florida, into the West, except Northwest ◦ FOOD Worms, slugs, salamanders, lizards, young snakes

→ LOOK FOR THIS
There are about a dozen varieties of the **RING-NECKED SNAKE**, with different ranges, different coloring, and differing amounts of black dots on their colorful undersides. Some experts consider some of these to be separate species.

FROM ABOVE, the Ring-necked Snake is quite plain, but underneath it's a whole different story. The brightly colored underside is a caution color in nature. The red-bellied variety of this snake is known to coil tightly when threatened, elevating its tail to expose a red tip in warning while hiding its head. These common woodland snakes spend much of their time in hiding.

GRAY, OLIVE, BROWN, OR BLACK BODY

ORANGE, YELLOW, OR CREAM NECK RING

UNDERSIDE IS RED, ORANGE, OR YELLOW WITH BLACK SPOTS.

10s spotters

Red-bellied Mudsnake

Farancia abacura LENGTH 3.3–4.6 ft (1–1.4 m) ◦ HABITAT Swamps, lake edges, sluggish streams, floodplains ◦ RANGE Southern Virginia to Florida, west to Texas, north through Mississippi Valley ◦ FOOD Salamanders, fish

THERE ARE A LOT OF RED-BELLIED MUDSNAKES out there, but it's very hard to see one because they often hide among water plants, bury themselves in the muddy bottoms of lakes or streams, or burrow into the soil. But you might see one crossing a road on a rainy night. The mudsnake has a sharp spine on the tip of its tail that it uses like an anchor when moving on slippery mud. Slimy salamanders are among its favorite foods.

RED OR PINK ON BELLY AND UP SIDES

10s spotters

BLACK SPOTS ON PALE CHIN AND NECK

GLOSSY BLACK OR GRAY BACK

Plains Hog-nosed Snake

Heterodon nasicus LENGTH 15–25 in (38–63 cm) • HABITAT Sandy and gravelly areas in scrub and grasslands • RANGE Plains from southern Canada through Arizona, New Mexico, and Texas into Mexico • FOOD Amphibians, rodents, lizards, insects

PLAYING DEAD is one of the Plains Hog-nosed Snake's go-to moves when it senses serious danger. It will coil belly-up, with its head thrown back and its mouth open and lie there motionless. If it is flipped over, it will immediately flop back into dead mode. Like other hog-noses, it produces venom that makes prey motionless. The venom does not affect humans very much, and this snake rarely bites.

UPTURNED NOSE THAT LOOKS LIKE A PIG'S SNOUT

BACK HAS BLOTCHES, SIDES HAVE SPOTS.

TAN, BROWN, OR GRAY BODY

Eastern Hog-nosed Snake

Heterodon platirhinos LENGTH 20–33 in (50–84 cm) • HABITAT Open woodlands, wooded hillsides, fields, meadows with sandy soil • RANGE Southern New England to Florida to Texas, north to South Dakota • FOOD Toads, other frogs

THE EASTERN HOG-NOSED SNAKE uses a number of dramatic fake-outs to fend off potential predators. In a signature move, the snake inflates its body with air, flattens its head and neck into a kind of cobra hood, hisses loudly—and then strikes. If that routine doesn't work, it may try the play-dead posture: belly up, head back, and mouth open. Some dark snakes have little or no pattern.

DARK SPOTS ON SIDES

DARK BLOTCHES ON BACK

UPTURNED NOSE

BROWN TO GRAY BODY

UNDERSIDE IS MOTTLED.

Plain-bellied Watersnake

Nerodia erythrogaster LENGTH 30–48 in (75–122 cm) ◦ HABITAT Rivers, streams, swamps, marshes, lakes, ditches, water tanks ◦ RANGE Most of eastern U.S., except Florida peninsula ◦ FOOD Frogs, fish

THE PLAIN-BELLIED WATERSNAKE isn't really plain. Adults may have no pattern, but their solid-color bodies are textured by keeled (ridged) scales, and their undersides are a solid red, orange, yellow, or cream. For a snake, the species has noticeably large eyes. Scientists think the eyes may help it see better when it watches for passing fish to catch. The Plain-belly often wanders far from water in hot weather and goes into forests to cool off.

→ LOOK FOR THIS
The **PLAIN-BELLIED WATERSNAKE** acts aggressively and opens its mouth when it's confronted, causing some people to mistake it for a venomous cottonmouth.

SOLID BROWN, OLIVE, OR REDDISH BODY

BACK SCALES HAVE KEELS, OR RIDGES.

LARGE EYES

UNDERSIDE IS RED, ORANGE, YELLOW, OR CREAM.

Southern Watersnake

Nerodia fasciata LENGTH 22–41 in (56–105 cm) ◦ HABITAT Freshwater and brackish habitats ◦ RANGE Coastal plain from North Carolina to Texas and Mississippi Valley ◦ FOOD Frogs, fish

WARM EVENING RAINS in the spring can bring multiple Southern Watersnakes out of the water in search of potential mates. Like other *Nerodia* species—and aquatic snakes in general—the female Southern Watersnake gives birth to live young that hatch from eggs inside her body. She usually gives birth in summer. She might have just a few babies or more than 50 at a time.

CROSSBANDS, OR NO PATTERN

BODY IS GRAY, TAN, OLIVE, OR BLACK.

MAY HAVE DARK LINE FROM EYE TO JAW

Common Watersnake

Nerodia sipedon LENGTH **22–41 in (56–105 cm)** • HABITAT **Freshwater and brackish habitats** • RANGE **Southern Ontario and Quebec, Canada, south to North Carolina, west to Mississippi and Colorado** • FOOD **Fish, amphibians, turtles, crustaceans, small mammals**

YOU MIGHT FIND a Common Watersnake sunning itself on banks or logs or casually hanging out on trees above water. When disturbed, it will quickly plop into the water. This snake has long teeth adapted for holding fish. Its saliva contains a substance that makes blood flow more freely, so after it bites, the prey bleeds quickly and dies. As this species gets older, its pattern typically darkens and becomes less noticeable. Because it is frequently covered with mud, it is often difficult to tell the Common Watersnake from the Southern one. When the Common Watersnake is annoyed, it will often flatten its body, discharge lots of musk, and may also poop.

EXPERT'S CIRCLE

DON'T BE FOOLED

The **COMMON WATERSNAKE** is often mistaken for a venomous cottonmouth, or water moccasin, and killed as a result. But the Common Watersnake has a different head shape, and it doesn't gape, or open its mouth wide, when disturbed.

BLOTCHES ON BACK AND SIDES

DARK BANDS ON NECK

BROWN, RED, GRAY, OR BLACK BODY

10s spotters

In which river are you sure to find snakes?

The Hiss-issippi!

Laugh Out Loud!

Graham's Crayfish Snake

Regina grahamii LENGTH 18–28 in (45–71 cm) ▪ HABITAT Ponds, streams, bayous, ditches ▪ RANGE Illinois and Iowa to Texas and Louisiana; northern Mississippi ▪ FOOD Crayfish, other crustaceans, amphibians, fish

LIKE OTHER CRAYFISH SNAKES,

Graham's Crayfish Snake likes its favorite prey to be freshly molted, meaning that the prey has shed its shell. It's easier to chomp down on a soft exoskeleton (outside covering) than a hard one. These snakes are common where crayfish, or crawdads, are plentiful. They even take shelter in the crawdad's mud-dribbled burrow, known as a chimney. Crayfish snakes also hide under rocks and debris. They bask on pond and stream banks and hang out in trees over water. These snakes tend to forage for food mostly at night during the summer heat. Females give birth to between 6 and 39 live young in late summer.

MAKE THIS!

Get an adult to help you boil two eggs, then use them to show the difference between reptile skin, which keeps moisture and air out, and amphibian skin, which lets moisture and air in.

1. Peel the shell off one egg.
2. Place both eggs in cups and cover them with water.
3. Put 8 drops of blue food coloring in both cups.
4. Wait 24 hours. Observe the eggs. Cut them in half.

Which egg took the color? Which one didn't? Can you tell which egg is like amphibian skin, letting moisture seep through?

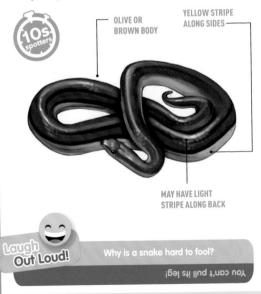

10s spotters

OLIVE OR BROWN BODY

YELLOW STRIPE ALONG SIDES

MAY HAVE LIGHT STRIPE ALONG BACK

Laugh Out Loud!

Why is a snake hard to fool?

You can't pull its leg!

Dekay's Brownsnake

Storeria dekayi LENGTH 9–13 in (23–33 cm) ◦ HABITAT Wetlands, moist woods, forests, urban areas ◦ RANGE Southern Minnesota; Quebec, Canada; and Maine south to Texas ◦ FOOD Earthworms, slugs, snails, insects

THIS CLOSE RELATIVE of the Red-bellied Snake chooses to live in places where lots of debris provides cover. In winter it may den in a group, sometimes in a building foundation. It often dens with other snake species. The female gives birth to 3 to 41 live young that often have a white ring around the neck. The babies hang around Mom for a short while, but she doesn't provide any care.

BACK STRIPE HAS A BORDER OF SMALL DARK SPOTS.

LIGHT STRIPE DOWN CENTER OF BACK

YELLOWISH, REDDISH, OR GRAYISH BROWN BODY

REPTILE file!

Even nonscientists make scientific discoveries! This snake's scientific name is *Storeria dekayi*. The first part, the genus, was named after David Humphreys Storer, because he was a respected New England doctor and amateur naturalist. James Ellsworth DeKay, a New York doctor, collected the first example, so the second part, the species, was named after him.

Red-bellied Snake

Storeria occipitomaculata LENGTH 8–16 in (20–40 cm) ◦ HABITAT Wooded hills and mountains, sphagnum bogs ◦ RANGE Extreme southeastern Saskatchewan, Canada, east and south through eastern U.S., except southern Florida ◦ FOOD Earthworms, slugs, insects

MANY SNAKES GAPE, or open their mouths wide, when threatened. The Red-bellied Snake has its own move: It curls its upper lip on one or both sides when disturbed. The Red-belly often is mistaken for Dekay's Brownsnake, until it shows its red belly. But not all Red-bellies have this feature. Some may have gray or blue-black undersides instead.

LIGHT STRIPE DOWN BACK

MAY HAVE 4 NARROW BROWN STRIPES DOWN BACK, WITH OR WITHOUT LIGHT STRIPE

BROWN, GRAY, OR BLACK BODY

OFTEN HAS RED BELLY

REPTILE REPORT
Venomous or Nonvenomous?

Warning Sign

Coralsnakes lack the head and eye shape of other kinds of venomous snakes. The warning sign is the color and position of their rings. These are different from those in nonvenomous ringed snakes. When red rings touch yellow ones, that's a warning sign. If red rings touch black, that's usually a sign that the snake is not venomous—at least in North America.

THE FOUR KINDS OF VENOMOUS SNAKES

—coralsnakes, rattlesnakes, cottonmouths, and copperheads—all produce a toxin in sacs inside their head that is delivered through fangs when they bite. The venom helps them kill their prey. Although venomous snakes might bite when threatened or frightened, most snakes avoid humans. Snakes would rather flee than fight—even the venomous ones! Still, it's important to be able to identify dangerous snakes. Here are some signs that a snake is venomous.

WHEN THREATENED, A COTTONMOUTH OPENS ITS MOUTH WIDE AND SHOWS OFF THE COTTON-WHITE INSIDES, AS WELL AS VENOM-FILLED FANGS IN ITS UPPER JAW.

Head's Up!

Head shape is a clue: Except for coralsnakes, venomous snakes, like this copperhead, have a head shaped like a triangle. Most nonvenomous snakes have a narrower head.

Eye Watch

The pupil of the eye is another clue: Venomous snakes have slitlike pupils, while most nonvenomous species have round pupils.

Warning Rattle

Rattlesnakes show the signature triangular head and slitlike pupil of a venomous snake. They also have special segments on the end of their tail that produce a warning rattle. This Western Diamond-backed Rattler is in defense mode, ready to strike to protect itself if it needs to.

Terrestrial Gartersnake

Thamnophis elegans LENGTH 18–43 in (46–109 cm) ▪ HABITAT Grasslands, woodlands, brushlands, desert, often near water ▪ RANGE Western United States and Canada ▪ FOOD Worms, slugs, snails, frogs, fish, small mammals

AS ITS NAME SUGGESTS, the Terrestrial Gartersnake spends a lot of its time on land. When danger threatens, it will often slither off into the brush, rather than head to the water and swim away. But it likes to live near ponds and lakes and hunts for frogs and fish. It paralyzes its prey by chewing a mild toxin into it. This toxin is not harmful to humans.

LIGHT STRIPE DOWN CENTER OF BACK

SIDES HAVE DARK MARKINGS.

BODY IS GRAY, OLIVE, OR BROWN.

OFTEN HAS THINNER LIGHT STRIPE ON SIDES

10s spotters

Checkered Gartersnake

Thamnophis marcianus LENGTH 18–24 in (46–60 cm) ▪ HABITAT Dry grasslands and sandy habitats near a water source ▪ RANGE Southeastern California, southern Arizona, and New Mexico to Texas, north to Kansas ▪ FOOD Frogs, fish, crayfish

THE CHECKERED GARTERSNAKE has—you guessed it!—checkerboard-patterned sides. The pattern may help conceal the snake by making its side stripes less noticeable so that it blends into its surroundings. Although this species lives where it's dry, it still depends on water, such as lakes, ponds, streams, and ditches, to provide its food, which includes frogs and other aquatic life.

10s spotters

BODY IS TAN, OLIVE, OR BROWN.

BACK HAS 3 LIGHT STRIPES.

BOLD CHECKERBOARD PATTERN ON SIDES

Western Ribbonsnake

Thamnophis proximus **LENGTH 18–48 in (46–120 cm)** •
HABITAT Edges of lakes, marshes, streams, ponds, ditches, water tanks
• **RANGE** Southern Wisconsin and Indiana through Mississippi Valley to
Texas and Louisiana • **FOOD** Frogs, salamanders, fish, lizards

RIBBONSNAKES ARE REALLY skinny
gartersnakes with longer tails that measure
about a third of their length. The Western
Ribbonsnake is known for often having an orange
stripe running down its back. This species, and
ribbonsnakes in general, usually spends more
time in the water than other gartersnakes do.
When it feels threatened—perhaps by a bird
or raccoon—it heads for the water and swims
among the plants on the surface. This habit
makes it different from a true watersnake,
which often will swim underwater. During rainy
weather, the Western Ribbonsnake may go to
shore in search of the frogs and salamanders
that form a big part of its diet.

→ LOOK FOR THIS
The **WESTERN RIBBONSNAKE**
is similar to the Eastern
Ribbonsnake *(T. sauritis)*,
but the Western often has
two colorful spots on top of
the head that touch. On the
Eastern Ribbonsnake, these
spots don't touch.

REPTILE file!

Snakes don't have eyelids, so
they never close their eyes.
They do have a clear scale
over each eye that protects it.
When a snake sheds its skin,
the eye scale comes off with
the rest of the skin and a new
one takes its place.

USUALLY HAS DULL ORANGE
STRIPE DOWN BACK

BODY IS BLACK, BROWN,
OLIVE, OR GRAY.

NO MARKINGS
ON UNDERSIDE

LIGHT STRIPE ON SIDES

10s
spotters

Common Gartersnake

Thamnophis sirtalis LENGTH 18–26 in (46–66 cm) • HABITAT Meadows, marshes, ditches, damp woods, urban areas, among others • RANGE Southern Canada and all of U.S., except desert Southwest • FOOD Amphibians, worms, small fish, mice

THE COMMON GARTERSNAKE lives all over southern Canada and throughout the United States—everywhere except some desert areas in the Southwest. This species comes in many varieties that have a basic look with a lot of small differences. Gartersnakes in general are known for their back and side stripes and often some kind of markings on the sides. There is also an all-black variety. They all act more or less the same and live in many different kinds of habitats. Some kinds spend more time in the water than others. Gartersnakes can put on a big show when they're annoyed or threatened. They flatten their bodies, strike, and discharge a smelly substance from the opening for waste on their underside.

REPTILE file!

Gartersnakes are very social snakes. Especially in the North, they brumate, or hibernate, in groups that can number in the thousands, often huddling together in a tangled mass. After mating in the spring, they usually go their separate ways. The females give birth a few months later to anywhere from 4 to 80 babies.

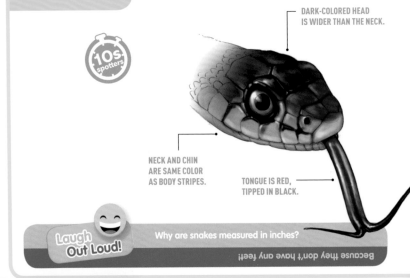

10s spotters

DARK-COLORED HEAD IS WIDER THAN THE NECK.

NECK AND CHIN ARE SAME COLOR AS BODY STRIPES.

TONGUE IS RED, TIPPED IN BLACK.

Laugh Out Loud! Why are snakes measured in inches?

Because they don't have any feet!

Lined Snake

Tropidoclonion lineatum LENGTH 8.5–15 in (22–38 in) • HABITAT Prairies, grasslands, woodland edges, suburban and urban areas • RANGE Scattered populations from South Dakota to Texas, west to New Mexico, east to Illinois • FOOD Mainly earthworms

THE LINED SNAKE is secretive and shy, so shy that scientists who study snakes probably don't know about all the places where it lives. There may be a lot more of them around than we think. Though shy, this snake adapts to living in many different kinds of habitats, including suburbs and cities, where it often hangs out in cemeteries. Spooky! These snakes often come out in the evening after warm rains to snag worms that come to the surface. In the winter, Lined Snakes brumate in the cracks and crevices of rocks or in animal burrows. They also spend time in cooler underground holes when it's very hot.

→ **LOOK FOR THIS**
The **LINED SNAKE** is related to the gartersnake. There are some differences. The lined snake is about half as long and has two rows of half-moon-shaped marks on its underside that gartersnakes don't have.

REPTILE file !

When threatened, the Lined Snake tightly coils its tail and hides its head inside the coil. It also may flatten its body. If captured, it may release a load of poop on its captor.

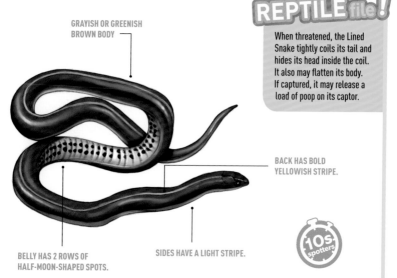

GRAYISH OR GREENISH BROWN BODY

BACK HAS BOLD YELLOWISH STRIPE.

BELLY HAS 2 ROWS OF HALF-MOON-SHAPED SPOTS.

SIDES HAVE A LIGHT STRIPE.

10s spotters

REPTILE REPORT
Snacking Snakes

A COMMON GARTERSNAKE USES EXCELLENT SMELL AND SIGHT TO FIND WORMS, FROGS, AND SMALL MAMMALS TO EAT.

SNAKES ARE KNOWN for their habit of pigging out on prey that is often larger than they are. A Common Gartersnake, for instance, might eat a worm or mouse that's wider than the snake's mouth or body. A Burmese Python can devour animals that are many times wider than its mouth or body. How is this possible? One thing that the snake does *not* do is detach its upper and lower jaws so that its mouth can fit around the mega meal, in spite of a common belief that it does. Read on for the real story.

Open Wide!

Snakes have flexible muscles and connectors called tendons and ligaments in their jaws that allow the jaws to stretch wide. The lower jaw is made up of two independently moving parts that are joined together by a ligament that stretches like a rubber band, allowing the jaw to get wider as the food is pulled in. Snakes also have a bone at the back of the head that moves aside to allow expansion.

Snake Walk

Once prey is captured, swallowing begins. The snake's jaws move, or "walk" over the prey, using the snake's teeth to pull it in. Ribs aren't attached to a breastbone, so the body can stretch and the windpipe can be extended like a snorkel so the snake can breathe as it swallows large prey.

Feeling Full

It can take days or even weeks for a snake to digest one large meal. This snake has been digesting a large animal for days. See the lump at the end of its tail? This meal might be enough to satisfy its hunger for months to come! Scientists have found that the warmer a snake's body is, the faster it digests its food. So a snake basking on a rock may be preparing for a big meal.

Smooth Earthsnake

Virginia valeriae LENGTH 7–10 in (18–25 cm) • HABITAT Woodlands, timbered slopes, grassy edges of streams and roads • RANGE New Jersey to northern Florida, west to eastern Kansas, Oklahoma, and Texas • FOOD Earthworms, soft insects

THE SMOOTH EARTHSNAKE might as well be called the Plain Earthsnake. It's a small snake with a solid, earthy color and few markings on its body. To make it even harder to notice, it's very secretive. It spends much of its time underground, burrowing in loose soil with its pointed snout. In times of drought, this snake digs deeper in search of moisture. It gets its food underground, too, eating mainly earthworms. When rains flood its underground burrows, both the snakes and the worms come to the surface. At times like those, the snakes look for other places to hide, such as under rocks or rotting logs or under trash and debris left by humans.

REPTILE file!

A baby Smooth Earthsnake does not hatch from an egg, but is born live from its mother's body. Like all newborn snakes, it is a miniature of its parents. It measures less than three inches (8 cm) long, which makes it easy for large spiders and beetles to take it as prey.

BODY IS GRAY OR REDDISH BROWN.

MAY HAVE FAINT LINE ON BACK

MAY HAVE LINE FROM EYE TO NOSTRIL

10s spotters

Arizona Coralsnake

Micruroides euryxanthus LENGTH 11–24.5 in (28–62 cm) ▪ HABITAT Arid scrublands, woodlands, grasslands, farmland ▪ RANGE Central and southern Arizona, southwestern New Mexico ▪ FOOD Lizards, snakes

THE ARIZONA CORALSNAKE is at home in many of the rocky and arid parts of the Southwest. Its flattened body shape suggests that it spends time in rock crevices. It comes out in the evening to hunt and will stay out quite late. It also comes out to hunt on overcast days because it's not too hot. Coralsnakes are dangerously venomous, but they're not very aggressive.

→ **LOOK FOR THIS**
Among U.S. snakes, you can tell if a ringed snake is venomous if it has white or yellow rings right next to the red ones like the **ARIZONA CORALSNAKE** does. If it has black next to red, like the milksnake, it's not venomous.

RED BANDS BORDERED BY YELLOW OR WHITE

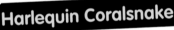

HEAD IS BLACK.

BLUNT SNOUT

Harlequin Coralsnake

Micrurus fulvius LENGTH 20–30 in (50–75 cm) ▪ HABITAT Sandy areas, pinewoods, pond and lake edges, hardwood hammocks ▪ RANGE North Carolina to southern Florida, along Gulf Coast to Louisiana, central Alabama ▪ FOOD Small snakes, lizards

AS WITH ALL CORALSNAKES, you can tell that the Harlequin Coralsnake is venomous by the position of its yellow and red "caution colors" next to each other. In nonvenomous snakes, yellow and red rings are separated by black. This snake is good at keeping itself hidden, using trash, leaves, bent grasses, fallen logs, or whatever is around to conceal itself. This species used to be called the Eastern Coralsnake.

BODY HAS WIDE RED AND BLACK RINGS SEPARATED BY NARROW YELLOW ONES.

HEAD IS BLACK.

Eastern Copperhead

Agkistrodon contortrix LENGTH 24–35 in (60–90 cm) ▪ HABITAT Rocky, wooded hillsides, swamp edges, mountainous areas ▪ RANGE Southern New England to northern Florida, west to eastern Texas and Oklahoma ▪ FOOD Rodents, lizards, frogs, large insects

A COPPERHEAD'S TRIANGULAR copper head shows that it is a pit viper, a venomous snake that has a heat-sensing opening, or pit, between its nostril and its eye. The pit provides this predator with pinpoint accuracy in detecting prey, even in the dark. It's so accurate that the snake doesn't have to use much energy to find a meal. It can just sit all coiled up, waiting for prey to wander by—then strike! When it feels threatened, a copperhead may vibrate its tail. Even though this snake has no rattle, the vibration makes a whirring sound in dry vegetation as a warning.

→ LOOK FOR THIS
YOUNG COPPERHEADS may have thin yellow or green tips on their tail. The bright color may serve as lures for lizards and frogs. These tips disappear as the snakes grow and mature.

DARK HOURGLASS BANDS ON BACK

TRIANGULAR COPPER HEAD

TAN OR BROWN BODY

Laugh Out Loud!
Knock, knock.
Who's there?
Snakeskin.
Snakeskin who?
Snakeskin bite, but they'd rather run away!

Northern Cottonmouth

Agkistrodon piscivorus LENGTH 30–47 in (75–120 cm) ▪ HABITAT Swamps, lakes, rivers, canals, rice fields ▪ RANGE Southeastern Virginia west to central Texas, north to Illinois, barely into northern Florida ▪ FOOD Amphibians, fish, snakes, birds

A CLOSE RELATIVE of copperheads, the Northern Cottonmouth is named for the cotton-white lining inside its mouth. The snake shows off the white lining—along with its fangs—by opening its mouth very wide in a defensive behavior that scientists call gaping. Because it is a pit viper, you should avoid all contact with any cottonmouth. Its venom is dangerous, and a bite can cause a serious infection. These snakes are mostly nocturnal, but they need to bask in the sun during the day to maintain their body temperature. They can be found on logs and stones by the edge of the water. Cottonmouths are also known as water moccasins.

→ **LOOK FOR THIS**

If you live in or visit an area where **COTTONMOUTHS** live, it's good to know the difference between cottonmouths and watersnakes (*Nerodia* genus). When disturbed, a nonvenomous watersnake tends to quickly slither or swim away. But a cottonmouth will often stand its ground by coiling and gaping, or it may slowly slither off. It may also vibrate its tail, which watersnakes do not do. Also, cottonmouths tend to swim with their head out of the water, while watersnakes usually swim under the water.

FLAT-TOPPED HEAD

DARK BAND THROUGH EYE

OLIVE, BROWN, OR BLACK BODY

BODY CAN BE PLAIN OR HAVE DARK CROSSBANDS.

REPTILE file !

Like all North American pit vipers, a cottonmouth bears live young. The babies are patterned and have yellow-tipped tails, much like young copperheads.

10s spotters

Eastern Diamond-backed Rattlesnake

Crotalus adamanteus LENGTH 33–71 in (84–180 cm) • HABITAT Saw palmetto, pine and oak woods, coastal areas • RANGE Southeastern North Carolina to Florida Keys and along Gulf of Mexico to eastern Texas • FOOD Rodents, other small mammals, birds

RATTLE ON TAIL

10s spotters

NORTH AMERICA'S largest rattlesnake, the Eastern Diamond-backed, is a snake to avoid. It gives warning that it's venomous with its rattle, made of loose interlocking segments on its tail. The buzzing noise the rattle makes sounds like the hum of cicadas. The Eastern Diamond-backed often lurks around Gopher Tortoise burrows, hoping to find an easy meal from the many small animals that take shelter in them.

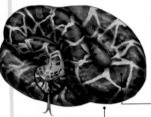

BACK HAS LARGE, DARK DIAMONDS BORDERED IN CREAM OR WHITE.

BODY IS BROWN OR BLACK.

Western Diamond-backed Rattlesnake

Crotalus atrox LENGTH 30–91 in (75–230 cm) • HABITAT Arid areas, including roadsides and vacant lots • RANGE Southwestern California to central Arkansas southward • FOOD Mammals, lizards, birds, amphibians

THE WESTERN DIAMOND-BACKED is a Hollywood star. Its scary rattle signals danger in many cowboy and Western films. In the southwestern states where it lives, the rattle warns grazing animals not to come too close or step on it. It injects a lot of strong venom with its bite. This species is sometimes called the coontail rattler because it has black and white or light gray bands on its tail, like a raccoon.

10s spotters

LARGE HEAD

BROWN, GRAY, OR PINKISH BODY

TAIL WITH RATTLE

Sidewinder

Crotalus cerastes LENGTH **17–33 in (43–84 cm)** • HABITAT **Arid desert with scrub-topped sand hammocks, dunes, hardpan, rocky slopes** • RANGE **Southern California to southwestern Utah southward** • FOOD **Small rodents, lizards, birds**

THE SIDEWINDER has a signature move. It makes an S-shaped motion that leaves a J-shaped track in the sand. This motion helps the rattlesnake travel through fine sand without slipping and also keeps it from making a lot of contact with hot sand. The Sidewinder spends its days the way other desert animals do: out of the sun. It hangs out in rodent burrows or in shallow depressions it may make at the base of shrubs. The Sidewinder also is often seen crossing roads in the desert at night.

→ **LOOK FOR THIS**
The **SIDEWINDER'S** rattle and the "horns" above its eyes give it the nickname "horned rattler." The horns seem to help protect the eyes from blowing desert sand or from falling dirt in underground burrows.

10s spotters

TAN, PINK, OR GRAY BODY

HORNLIKE SCALES ABOVE EYES

BACK HAS BLOTCHES.

Laugh Out Loud!

What did the naughty rattlesnake say to his sister?

Don't be such a rattle-tail!

Timber Rattlesnake

Crotalus horridus LENGTH 36–60 in (90–152 cm) • HABITAT
Woodlands, rocky hillsides, swamps, stream valleys • RANGE
Southern Maine to northern Florida, west to Texas and Minnesota •
FOOD Rodents, birds

DESPITE HAVING A SPECIES name that includes the word "horrid," the Timber Rattlesnake is one of the calmer rattlers. If disturbed, it may not make any aggressive move, but it should still be left alone. The Timber Rattlesnake is an ambush predator. It stays quietly coiled and waiting in a place where prey animals often pass by. When one does, it attacks swiftly. The snake's venom kills the victim quickly. That allows the snake to eat it slowly, since it isn't wriggling to escape. In winter, Timber Rattlers brumate in communal dens, called hibernacula, often in the company of copperheads. The species is found in greater numbers in the South, where it is known as the Canebrake Rattlesnake.

→ **LOOK FOR THIS**
TIMBER RATTLESNAKE
males challenge each other by performing "combat dances." Two males slither up to each other and wrestle side by side. They writhe and roll around, performing this "dance" repeatedly until one of them tires—and slithers away.

REPTILE file!

When a rattlesnake sheds its skin, it grows another segment on its rattle. But older rattlesnakes don't end up with superlong rattles because segments frequently break off.

MAY HAVE A STRIPE
DOWN MIDDLE ON BACK

BODY IS YELLOW, BROWN, GRAY, TAN, OR PINKISH.

BACK HAS BLOTCHES OR CROSSBANDS.

TAIL IS DARK.

Prairie Rattlesnake

Crotalus viridis LENGTH 35–45 in (89–114 cm) • HABITAT **Grasslands, dunes, forests, rocky areas** • RANGE **Great Plains of U.S. and Canada** • FOOD **Small mammals, birds**

THE PRAIRIE RATTLESNAKE in the Great Plains is much like the Timber Rattlesnake in the East. But it has a much more aggressive personality than the Timber Rattlesnake and delivers an even more venomous bite. Even though the species can benefit farmers and ranchers by eating rodents, it has been hunted and killed for centuries for killing people and livestock. People also destroy the hibernacula, or places where these rattlesnakes hibernate, or brumate, in large groups. The rattlers often use ready-made mammal burrows for brumation or winter in a den on a rocky ledge or slope that faces south for warmth. The Prairie Rattler often hangs around prairie dog towns, which provide shelter—and often a meal.

→ **LOOK FOR THIS**
You can tell the **PRAIRIE RATTLESNAKE** from the Western Diamond-backed Rattlesnake by the black and white rings around the tail of the Prairie Rattlesnake.

REPTILE file!

Prairie Rattlesnakes are creatures of habit. They like to use the same hibernacula (communal dens) year after year. This makes it easier for scientists to find out where the rattlesnakes live and to study their populations. This way scientists can learn about rattler behavior and how to protect their habitat.

BROWN OR BLACK BLOTCHES ON BACK

BODY IS GREENISH, GRAY, OR BROWN.

Pygmy Rattlesnake

Sistrurus miliarius LENGTH 15–21 in (38–53 cm) • HABITAT Wet prairies, palmetto-pine woods, mixed forests, lakes, marshes • RANGE South Carolina through Florida, west to eastern Texas and Oklahoma • FOOD Amphibians, lizards, rodents, snakes

KNOWN AS A GROUND RATTLER, the Pygmy Rattlesnake has a slender tail and a mini-rattle that makes a sound like a buzzing insect. The body color of this snake varies a lot. It can be tan, gray, brown, black, reddish—or even lavender! In the past, the species used to be found around the piles of sawdust and bark at sawmills. These days, it hangs around dumps and lots filled with trash. This species also likes to warm itself along country roads in the evenings. It might be small compared to other rattlesnakes, but the Pygmy Rattlesnake still produces strong venom and a dangerous bite.

→ **LOOK FOR THIS**
Unlike the **RATTLESNAKES** in the genus *Crotalus*, which have small scales on the top of their head, the Pygmy Rattlesnake and its relatives have nine large scales. Also, its rattle sound is very faint compared to other rattlesnakes.

10s spotters

BODY COLOR IS TAN, GRAY, BROWN, REDDISH, BLACK, OR LAVENDER.

BACK HAS DARK BLOTCHES.

SIDES HAVE 2 TO 3 ROWS OF SPOTS.

What does a well-dressed snake wear?

Laugh Out Loud!

A boa tie!

Eastern Hellbender

Cryptobranchus alleganiensis LENGTH 11.5–20 in (29–50 cm)
• HABITAT Fast-flowing clear streams with rocky bottoms • RANGE New York to Georgia west to Missouri and Arkansas • FOOD Crayfish, other invertebrates

THE EASTERN HELLBENDER is so slimy that it's sometimes called a "snot otter." Because it is aquatic, nocturnal, and secretive, this mega-salamander doesn't get a lot of face time with humans, which explains the many myths and legends about North America's largest salamander. But the species is not aggressive or venomous, as some people think. It's just big—about as long as a dachshund! The population of hellbenders has declined a lot because of pollution, the silting of streams from erosion, and sand and gravel mining, which disturbs its watery habitat.

AMPHIBfile!

The male Eastern Hellbender is a very attentive dad. Smaller than the female, he gets involved before the first egg is even laid. He makes a nest cavity under a rock or log for the female to lay her eggs. Then he protects the eggs until they hatch in about three months.

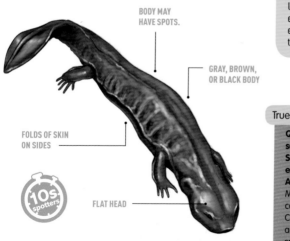

BODY MAY HAVE SPOTS.

GRAY, BROWN, OR BLACK BODY

FOLDS OF SKIN ON SIDES

10s spotters

FLAT HEAD

True or False

Q: There are no salamanders in the Great Smoky Mountains of the eastern United States.
A: False. The Great Smoky Mountains have been called the Salamander Capital of the World. The area has more than 30 species of salamanders.

Common Mudpuppy

Necturus maculosus LENGTH 8–13 in (20–33 cm) • HABITAT Lakes, ponds, streams • RANGE Great Lakes region south to Missouri and Alabama • FOOD Crayfish, other invertebrates, small fish

THE COMMON MUDPUPPY never fully changes from a larval, or immature, form into an adult, but it can reproduce. This aquatic salamander keeps the larval lifestyle, along with its frilly maroon gills, throughout its life. Never leaving the water, it hides among rocks, logs, and plants on the bottom of ponds or streams and comes out at night to feed. The Common Mudpuppy is one of the few salamanders that make noise. It's not much of a noise, just a high-pitched squeak. But it reminded some people of a dog's bark and became the source of the salamander's common name.

AMPHIB file!

At breeding time, female Common Mudpuppies lay between 30 and 190 eggs at a time, which they attach one by one under rocks. Like other salamanders, they guard the eggs until they hatch about five to nine weeks later.

→ LOOK FOR THIS
The length of the **COMMON MUDPUPPY'S** gills is related to the temperature and clarity of the water in which the salamander lives. The warmer and muddier the water, the longer the gills it will grow.

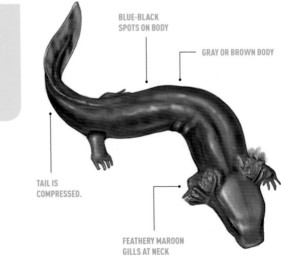

BLUE-BLACK SPOTS ON BODY

GRAY OR BROWN BODY

TAIL IS COMPRESSED.

FEATHERY MAROON GILLS AT NECK

10s spotters

Lesser Siren

Siren intermedia LENGTH 7–27 in (18–68 cm) • HABITAT Swamps, ponds, ditches • RANGE Southeastern Virginia to Florida, Gulf Coast to Texas, north along Mississippi Valley to Michigan • FOOD Aquatic invertebrates, small fish

THE EEL-LIKE LESSER SIREN looks like something out of a prehistoric swamp. It has very small forelegs and no hind legs and it keeps its gills throughout its life. With only two legs to use, the Lesser Siren doesn't have the option to relocate when its pond dries up in hot weather. It may hunker down in the muddy pond bottom. When that dries out, this salamander can secrete, or discharge, a protective covering around its body and wait for rain. The species is one of the rare salamanders that make noise. The sounds it makes include clicks and shrill yelps.

GRAY, OLIVE, OR BLACK BODY

MAY HAVE BLACK SPOTTING

SMALL FRONT LEGS HAVE 4 TOES.

10S spotters

MAKE THIS!

To get a better look at pond life, including slippery salamanders, make this milk-carton pond viewer. It's super easy!

1. Rinse out a half-gallon milk carton.
2. Use scissors to cut off the top and bottom.
3. Stretch a piece of plastic wrap tightly over one end.
4. Keep it in place with several rubber bands.
5. At the edge of a shallow pond or stream (be careful!), put the covered end into the water and peer in. What do you see?

Two-toed Amphiuma

Amphiuma means LENGTH 14–30 in (35–75 cm) • HABITAT Streams, lakes, bayous, wet meadows, ditches • RANGE Southeastern Virginia to Florida, west along Gulf Coast to Louisiana • FOOD Crayfish, other invertebrates, frogs, salamanders

AMPHIB file!

The female Two-toed Amphiuma lays her eggs under logs, rocks, and other objects in damp places or sometimes in shallow water or underground. She creates a shallow hole and deposits the eggs in a beadlike chain. Then she lies down to guard the eggs. They hatch one or two months later.

THE LARGE TWO-TOED AMPHIUMA has an eel-like body and two sets of tiny, useless limbs. It likes to live in bodies of water with muddy bottoms, so it can have a place to hide during the day. Despite its nonfunctional legs, this salamander can leave the water. It moves slowly over moist ground and sometimes can be found hiding under objects at the water's edge. A nickname for this species is "conger eel."

10s spotters

LARGE HEAD WITH ROUND, LIDLESS EYES

EACH OF 4 TINY LIMBS HAS 2 TOES.

BODY IS BROWN OR BLACK ABOVE, GRAY UNDERNEATH.

Three-toed Amphiuma

Amphiuma tridactylum LENGTH 18–30 in (45–75 cm) • HABITAT Lakes, marshes, streams, swamps, ditches • RANGE Missouri and Kentucky south to Texas, Louisiana, Mississippi, Alabama • FOOD Invertebrates, fish, snakes, amphibians

THE THREE-TOED AMPHIUMA is one of three *Amphiuma* species in the United States. They differ by whether they have one, two, or three toes. This species lives mainly in the Mississippi Delta region and likes to live in muddy waters with lots of vegetation. Its slim and slimy body moves through the water like an eel. It sometimes emerges from the water at night to feed.

UNDERSIDE IS LIGHT.

10s spotters

4 SLIM LIMBS WITH 3 TOES

BODY IS GRAY, BLACK, OR BROWN ABOVE.

Red-spotted Newt

Notopthalmus viridescens LENGTH 2.25–4.75 in (6–12 cm) • HABITAT Ponds, lakes, quiet streams, moist woodlands • RANGE Southeastern Canada and eastern U.S. • FOOD Invertebrates, young amphibians, amphibian eggs

THE AQUATIC RED-SPOTTED NEWT usually goes through a land-based stage of life in between its aquatic larval (immature) and adult forms. At this stage, it looks like an adult but has a brilliant red color. That's why it's called a Red Eft. An eft is an immature newt. On land it can wander away from water. Sooner or later, the eft returns to a wet home, where it morphs into an aquatic adult capable of reproducing.

SMOOTH ADULT BODY IS BROWN TO GREEN.

BACK HAS BLACK-CIRCLED RED SPOTS.

BODY HAS SMALL BLACK SPECKS.

Rough-skinned Newt

Taricha granulosa LENGTH 2.25–3.6 in (6–9 cm) • HABITAT Ponds, lakes, slow-moving streams, moist forests, grasslands • RANGE Pacific Coast from southeastern Alaska to Northern California • FOOD Invertebrates

DANGER!

The Rough-skinned Newt secretes a highly toxic substance through its skin, similar to the toxin in pufferfish. This seems to protect the newt as it roams about during the day. When a predator threatens, the newt curls its tail toward its head, displaying its colorful underside as a warning.

THROUGHOUT THE YEAR, it's breeding time for some Rough-skinned Newts. When the male Rough-skinned Newt goes courting in ponds and streams, his warty skin becomes much smoother. It seems the females prefer smooth guys! The females, which stay rough-skinned, lay their eggs one at a time on plants under the water. This species might have been brought by humans into Idaho and Montana, where they've started small populations.

WARTY BODY IS TAN, BROWN, OR BLACK ABOVE.

UNDERSIDE IS YELLOW TO ORANGE.

Blue-spotted Salamander

Ambystoma laterale LENGTH 3.5–5.5 in (9–14 cm) ▪ HABITAT Woodlands, coniferous forests, swamps, small ponds ▪ RANGE Eastern and south-central Canada and Great Lakes region of U.S. ▪ FOOD Insects, spiders, other small invertebrates

AMPHIB file !

When the Blue-spotted Salamander feels threatened, it uses defensive moves. It may wave its tail and ooze a yucky white fluid from the tail's base. If that doesn't work, the tail may drop off and wriggle—allowing the salamander to escape.

WHEN A BLUE-SPOTTED SALAMANDER has a lot of blue spots, it can look like the surface of a speckled enamel bowl. This secretive, nocturnal salamander lives in the leaf litter on the forest floor or uses the underground burrows of other animals. It comes out to breed after the snow melts, which makes temporary breeding pools in spring.

BLUE OR TURQUOISE SPOTS ON SIDES, TAIL, AND LEGS

12 RIB GROOVES

BODY IS SHINY GRAY OR BLUE-BLACK.

Long-toed Salamander

Ambystoma macrodactylum ▪ LENGTH 1.6–3.5 in (4–9 cm) ▪ HABITAT Sagebrush, grasslands, damp forests, mountain meadows, rocky shores of lakes ▪ RANGE Southeastern Alaska to northeastern California, east to Idaho, north to western Alberta, Canada ▪ FOOD Insects, other invertebrates

→ LOOK FOR THIS
A good time to look for **LONG-TOED SALAMANDERS** is after the snow melts in early spring. These are one of the first salamanders to emerge for breeding. They're often found hiding under logs near the edges of ponds and streams.

IT COMES AS NO SURPRISE that the Long-toed Salamander is known for its four long toes on each foot, one toe longer than the rest. This species belongs to the group of mole salamanders that burrow underground and spend a lot of their lives there. The Long-toed Salamander lives in a variety of habitats and at elevations ranging from sea level to 9,000 feet (2,700 m).

12–13 RIB GROOVES ON SIDES

YELLOW STRIPE OR PATTERN OF BLOTCHES ON BACK

DARK BROWN OR BLACK BODY

Spotted Salamander

Ambystoma maculatum LENGTH 4.3–7.25 in (11–18 cm) • HABITAT Moist, mixed woodlands near ponds, streams, temporary pools • RANGE Southeastern Canada south to Texas and Georgia • FOOD Insects, other invertebrates

THE SPOTTED SALAMANDER is difficult to spot above ground. It's a mole salamander and spends much of its time hiding under logs or in the burrows of other animals. This species comes out at night to hunt for insects. In the spring, Spotted Salamanders head to pools of water, where they breed. The large, round eggs that the females lay start out clear but turn green when they absorb algae.

BODY IS GRAY, BLUE-BLACK, OR BLACK.

HAS 2 ROWS OF ORANGE-YELLOW SPOTS FROM HEAD TO TAIL

USUALLY HAS 12 RIB GROOVES

10s spotters

Marbled Salamander

Ambystoma opacum LENGTH 3.5–4.25 in (9–11 cm) • HABITAT Woodlands, floodplains • RANGE Southern New England to northern Florida, west to Texas, north to Wisconsin • FOOD Insects, other invertebrates

The white or gray patterns on the shiny black body of the Marbled Salamander make it look like it might blend in pretty well if you placed it on a marble kitchen counter. There's a greater chance of seeing this species out and about above the ground than there is for other mole salamanders. And unlike other *Ambystoma* salamanders that breed and lay eggs in water, this species lays its eggs in the fall on land near water.

10s spotters

WHITE OR GRAY PATTERNS ON BACK

BODY IS SHINY BLACK.

HEAD HAS BLUNT SHAPE.

Eastern Tiger Salamander

Ambystoma tigrinum LENGTH **7–8.25 in (18–21 cm)** · HABITAT **Pine barrens, woodlands, meadows** · RANGE **Mid-Atlantic, southeastern and central U.S., except southern Appalachians and lower Mississippi Delta** · FOOD **Invertebrates, amphibians, small mammals**

THE EASTERN TIGER SALAMANDER has landed on the endangered species list in a number of U.S. states. This salamander has a hard time finding the right kind of habitat it needs when building projects and roads take those places away. Physically, the Eastern Tiger Salamander is stout and sturdy—one of the largest land salamanders in the world. Like the tiger, it's a fierce predator, hunting insects, frogs, and even other salamanders at night. To find shelter, it takes over burrows of other animals or digs its own up to two feet (0.6 m) below the surface.

AMPHIB file!

The Eastern Tiger Salamander breeds very early in the spring, often in deeper water than other salamanders. The female lays masses of eggs that attach to debris in the water.

10s spotters

BROWN OR BLACK BODY

YELLOWISH SPOTS ON BACK THAT MAY EXTEND DOWN SIDES

EXPERT'S CIRCLE

DON'T BE FOOLED The **WESTERN TIGER SALAMANDER** *(Ambystoma mavortium)* doesn't always have tigerlike looks. It sometimes has patterns of spots or bars on a cream or yellow body. It lives in the western United States and Canada, but it is not widespread in Nevada and California.

California Giant Salamander

Dicamptodon ensatus LENGTH 2.5–6.7 in (6–17 cm) ◦ HABITAT Rivers, cool, moist forests ◦ RANGE California ◦ FOOD Invertebrates, mice, snakes, other salamanders

THE CALIFORNIA GIANT SALAMANDER normally hides under rocks and logs and in burrows along stream banks. But sometimes it is spotted walking on the forest floor or crossing roads during rains. This large predator eats many different kinds of small animals, from insects to mice to snakes. Its aquatic larvae are also fierce predators. They act like cannibals, eating smaller larvae of their own species, as well as going after frog tadpoles. All this predatory activity makes them the most common amphibians in some streams. Sometimes the larvae never transform into adults that live on land, but continue to have gills and live underwater.

AMPHIB file !

The California Giant Salamander is one of a few salamanders that make noise. When it's grabbed or annoyed in some way, it may make low-pitched barking sounds.

DANGER!

No matter how cool it looks, do not try to handle a California Giant Salamander. If it gets defensive, it can inflict a painful bite.

BODY IS BROWN TO PURPLISH.

BODY HAS DARK MOTTLING.

SKIN IS SMOOTH.

10s spotters

Green Salamander

Aneides aeneus **LENGTH** 3.5–5 in (9–13 cm) • **HABITAT** Rock crevices in sandstone, under bark • **RANGE** Southwestern Pennsylvania through mountains to Alabama • **FOOD** Ants, mosquitoes, other invertebrates

WHEN YOU'RE A SALAMANDER that lives in damp rocks among lichens and mosses, it helps to look like those kinds of plant life. The Green Salamander has large patches of green on its body that really help it blend in. This species often brumates, or hibernates, in a group in rock crevices on cliff faces. When winter is over, the salamanders go back to living alone. At breeding time, male Green Salamanders often get into fights, shoving and biting each other. The female uses strands of mucus to attach her clutch of 10 to 20 eggs to the upper surfaces of rock crevices. When the babies hatch, they look like miniature adults. This species doesn't go through a stage as a water-dwelling larva.

AMPHIB file!

Like many salamander species, the female Green Salamander guards her eggs after she lays them. She lies next to them or coils around them until they hatch. The young stay in the crevice for a couple of months before they go out on their own.

10s spotters

BODY IS BROWN OR BLACK ABOVE.

TOES ARE SQUARED.

LARGE GREEN PATCHES ON BACK

Laugh Out Loud!

What do you call a lying salamander?

An am-FIB-ian!

California Slender Salamander

Batrachoseps attenuatus LENGTH 3–5.5 in (8–14 cm) •
HABITAT Hardwood and coniferous forests, grasslands • RANGE
Northern California, southwestern Oregon • FOOD Mites, spiders, other
invertebrates

THIS WORMLIKE SALAMANDER doesn't see
much of the Northwest scenery where it
lives. It often spends most of its life in an area
only about six feet (1.8 m) in diameter. There, it
lives under leaves, rotting logs, and rocks. It lies
in wait for small invertebrates, such as insects,
spiders, and mites. At breeding time, the female
may go into earthworm or termite burrows to
lay 5 to 20 eggs. Other females may add their
eggs to the nest, but the moms don't stay
around to guard them. In two or three months,
the babies hatch as mini-adults that breathe
through their skin. Like Green Salamanders, the
young skip the water-dwelling larva stage.

AMPHIBfile!

When it feels threatened and
goes into defensive mode, the
California Slender Salamander
doesn't do anything too fancy.
It may coil up and remain still
and then uncoil quickly and
sprint away. As with other
salamanders (and lizards), the
tail may detach and wriggle
to distract a predator.

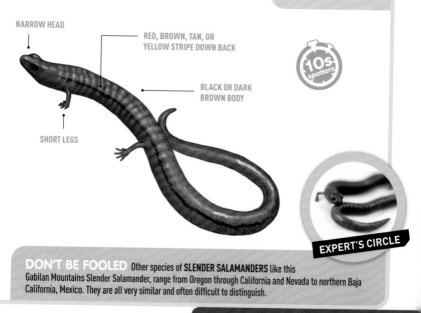

NARROW HEAD

RED, BROWN, TAN, OR
YELLOW STRIPE DOWN BACK

BLACK OR DARK
BROWN BODY

SHORT LEGS

10s
spotters

EXPERT'S CIRCLE

DON'T BE FOOLED Other species of **SLENDER SALAMANDERS** like this
Gabilan Mountains Slender Salamander, range from Oregon through California and Nevada to northern Baja
California, Mexico. They are all very similar and often difficult to distinguish.

Northern Dusky Salamander

Desmognathus fuscus LENGTH 2.5–4.5 in (6–11 cm) • HABITAT Rocky creeks, seeps, springs, flood plains, temporary channels • RANGE Southeastern Canada to Kentucky, Tennessee, and Georgia • FOOD Invertebrates, salamanders

THE NORTHERN DUSKY SALAMANDER belongs to a group of dusky salamanders that look a lot like each other and have ranges that often overlap. To make it even trickier to tell them apart, different species of dusky salamander often hang out together. The Northern Dusky Salamander also likes the company of the Northern Red Salamander. The Northern Dusky is a pretty common species, but it will scurry away if discovered, diving under leaf litter. The mottling or speckling on the body in this group of salamanders often becomes less noticeable as the animals age.

AMPHIB file !

The female Northern Dusky Salamander lays clusters of grape-like eggs on the edges of land near water. She tends to stay away from streams with hungry fish. She stays with the eggs for six to ten weeks until they hatch into aquatic larvae. The larvae then spend about a year in the water until they morph into adults that live on land.

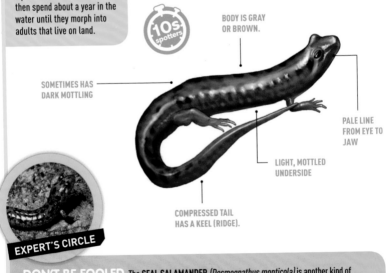

10s spotters

BODY IS GRAY OR BROWN.

SOMETIMES HAS DARK MOTTLING

PALE LINE FROM EYE TO JAW

LIGHT, MOTTLED UNDERSIDE

COMPRESSED TAIL HAS A KEEL (RIDGE).

EXPERT'S CIRCLE

DON'T BE FOOLED The **SEAL SALAMANDER** *(Desmognathus monticola)* is another kind of dusky salamander that lives in a portion of the same range as the Northern Dusky Salamander. The Seal is usually longer and heavier than the Northern Dusky and its underside lacks mottling.

Ensatina

Ensatina eschscholtzii LENGTH 1.5–3.5 in (4–9 cm) ◦ HABITAT
Moist woodlands, shady canyons, grasslands, chaparral ◦ RANGE
**Southern British Columbia, Canada, south to northern Baja California,
Mexico** ◦ FOOD **Insects, other invertebrates**

UNLIKE MANY OTHER WOODLAND
salamanders, the Ensatina doesn't go
through an aquatic larval stage. Instead,
the female lays eggs underground and then
cares for them to keep them moist until they
hatch. This salamander comes in a variety of
colors and patterns that differ according to
where the salamander lives. The basic Ensatina
color is brown or black. Some are plain brown,
but others have patterns in yellow, orange, or
cream. Some experts think that some of the
subspecies are really separate species. Like
other salamanders without lungs, the Ensatina
breathes through its skin.

AMPHIB file !

When threatened, an Ensatina
may stand stiff-legged, with
its back arched like a dome,
and swing its tail. If the tail is
grabbed, it may break off at
the narrow base. The Ensatina
also secretes a yucky, milky
liquid from the tail that helps
fend off predators.

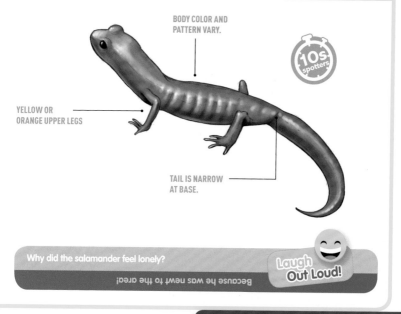

BODY COLOR AND
PATTERN VARY.

10s
spotters

YELLOW OR
ORANGE UPPER LEGS

TAIL IS NARROW
AT BASE.

Why did the salamander feel lonely?

Because he was newt to the area!

Laugh
Out Loud!

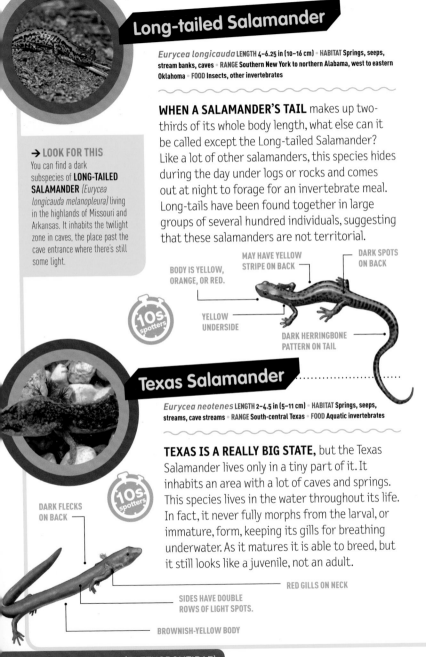

Long-tailed Salamander

Eurycea longicauda LENGTH 4–6.25 in (10–16 cm) • HABITAT Springs, seeps, stream banks, caves • RANGE Southern New York to northern Alabama, west to eastern Oklahoma • FOOD Insects, other invertebrates

WHEN A SALAMANDER'S TAIL makes up two-thirds of its whole body length, what else can it be called except the Long-tailed Salamander? Like a lot of other salamanders, this species hides during the day under logs or rocks and comes out at night to forage for an invertebrate meal. Long-tails have been found together in large groups of several hundred individuals, suggesting that these salamanders are not territorial.

→ **LOOK FOR THIS**
You can find a dark subspecies of **LONG-TAILED SALAMANDER** *(Eurycea longicauda melanopleura)* living in the highlands of Missouri and Arkansas. It inhabits the twilight zone in caves, the place past the cave entrance where there's still some light.

MAY HAVE YELLOW STRIPE ON BACK

DARK SPOTS ON BACK

BODY IS YELLOW, ORANGE, OR RED.

YELLOW UNDERSIDE

DARK HERRINGBONE PATTERN ON TAIL

Texas Salamander

Eurycea neotenes LENGTH 2–4.5 in (5–11 cm) • HABITAT Springs, seeps, streams, cave streams • RANGE South-central Texas • FOOD Aquatic invertebrates

TEXAS IS A REALLY BIG STATE, but the Texas Salamander lives only in a tiny part of it. It inhabits an area with a lot of caves and springs. This species lives in the water throughout its life. In fact, it never fully morphs from the larval, or immature, form, keeping its gills for breathing underwater. As it matures it is able to breed, but it still looks like a juvenile, not an adult.

DARK FLECKS ON BACK

RED GILLS ON NECK

SIDES HAVE DOUBLE ROWS OF LIGHT SPOTS.

BROWNISH-YELLOW BODY

Spring Salamander

Gyrinophilus porphyriticus LENGTH 4.75–7.5 in (12–19 cm)
◦ HABITAT Springs, clear streams, seeps ◦ RANGE New England through Appalachians to Alabama and Georgia ◦ FOOD Invertebrates, small salamanders

THE SPRING SALAMANDER isn't named for the season, it's named for its preferred habitat. This salamander has no lungs, and it needs water with a lot of oxygen to be able to breathe through its skin. Springs provide an ideal home. The Spring Salamander is active year-round at night, coming out to forage for invertebrates on land and in the water. It sometimes preys on other salamanders. By day it hides under rocks at stream edges. After the fall and winter breeding season, the female lays 40 to 60 eggs in the spring under stones and logs and protects them until they hatch in the summer.

AMPHIB file!

Spring Salamanders are in no hurry to morph from their immature larval form into adult form. They may spend up to four years as larvae with gills, living totally in the water. Their genus name, *Gyrinophilus*, means "tadpole lover" for the long time spent as larvae.

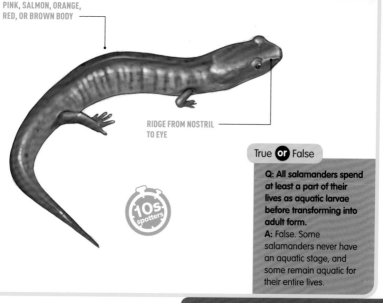

PINK, SALMON, ORANGE, RED, OR BROWN BODY

RIDGE FROM NOSTRIL TO EYE

10s spotters

True or False

Q: All salamanders spend at least a part of their lives as aquatic larvae before transforming into adult form.
A: False. Some salamanders never have an aquatic stage, and some remain aquatic for their entire lives.

Mud Salamander

Pseudotriton montanus LENGTH 3–6.5 in (8–17 cm) • HABITAT Muddy streams, springs, bogs, swamps • RANGE Southern New Jersey through northern Florida, along Gulf Coast to Louisiana • FOOD Insects, spiders, other small invertebrates

AS THE NAME SUGGESTS, the Mud Salamander is at home in murky and muddy streams and springs. It also likes to take over crayfish burrows, which are made of dribbled mud, like little sand castles. It doesn't require the clear waters that some other salamander species prefer. The female lays her eggs in water or on land every other year. She tends to lay a lot of eggs at one time, up to about 190. The eggs hatch into larvae that morph into adult form when they're about 18 months old. As this species ages, its coloring gets muddier and its spots become less distinct.

→ LOOK FOR THIS
The **MUD SALAMANDER** resembles the Red Salamander (next page), and their ranges overlap. Experts can have trouble telling them apart, although eye color (brown for Mud, yellow for Red) is often a reliable way to tell which is which.

SEPARATE ROUND BLACK SPOTS, NOT CLOSELY SPACED

BODY IS RED OR BROWN.

BROWN EYE

AMPHIBfile!

Mud Salamanders don't mind the cold as much as many other salamander species do. They've even been seen going about their daily lives in ice-draped streams.

Red Salamander

Pseudotriton ruber **LENGTH 4–6 in (10–15 cm)** • **HABITAT Woodlands, swamps, meadows with springs and streams** • **RANGE Southern New York southeast to Gulf Coast in Florida, Alabama, and Mississippi** • **FOOD Earthworms, other invertebrates**

RED SALAMANDERS prefer to live in water that is clean and clear. They usually avoid muddy water. They belong to a large group of lungless salamanders that breathe through their skin and the linings of their mouths. The Red Salamander captures prey such as insects and worms with a projectile tongue. The tongue can extend and return to the salamander's mouth in only 11 milliseconds! Female Reds lay 30 to 130 eggs underground, attached to rocks in places where water seeps to the surface. The eggs hatch into larvae in late fall or early winter. The young remain in this form up to three years, before transforming into adults.

→ **LOOK FOR THIS**
The best time to look for **RED SALAMANDERS** is at night, when they hunt. But you can still find them during the day. Look for their bright orange-red color, which fades as they age. Also find their irregular spots.

MAKE THIS!

By rolling logs, you can make a study of the critters that live underneath—including salamanders. Stand on one side of the log and roll it very slowly and carefully toward you so you don't harm any animals underneath. Keep your eyes on the exposed ground, as some animals may run off quickly in the opposite direction. When you've seen all there is to see, slowly roll the log back into its original position.

BODY IS RED TO ORANGE-RED WITH MANY ROUNDED BLACK SPOTS.

EYE IS YELLOW.

10s spotters

Four-toed Salamander

Hemidactylium scutatum LENGTH 2–3.5 in (5–9 cm) • HABITAT Bogs, streams, woodlands with sphagnum moss • RANGE Separated populations, mostly east of the Mississippi River, from Nova Scotia, Canada, to the Florida Panhandle, except southern Atlantic coast • FOOD Invertebrates

TO IDENTIFY A FOUR-TOED SALAMANDER, check out the feet. This species has four toes on the front and hind feet, while most salamanders have five toes on the hind feet. The Four-toed Salamander breeds in late winter or early spring, often on rainy evenings. The female attaches her 30 to 50 eggs to sphagnum moss near the water's edge. She stays near the eggs to protect them. When the eggs hatch, the larvae wiggle toward the water, where, hopefully, there are no fish to eat them up upon arrival.

AMPHIB file!

The male Four-toed Salamander is smaller than the female and has a tail that is longer in comparison with its body.

10s. spotters

→ **LOOK FOR THIS**
The **FOUR-TOED SALAMANDER** shows a narrowing around the base of its tail. This is where the tail breaks off when it's grabbed. The tail will wriggle by itself while the salamander has a chance to get away.

CONSTRICTION, OR NARROWING, AT BASE OF TAIL

BODY IS REDDISH BROWN WITH GRAY SIDES.

WHITE UNDERSIDE WITH SPOTS

4 TOES ON EACH FOOT

Eastern Red-backed Salamander

Plethodon cinereus LENGTH 2.5–4 in (6–10 cm) • HABITAT Wooded ravines, hillsides, woodlands • RANGE Southern Canada and Minnesota south to North Carolina • FOOD Invertebrates

THE EASTERN RED-BACKED SALAMANDER isn't one of a kind. It's one of many similar and closely related woodland salamanders that were once thought to be a single species spread out over a huge area. Members of this group of small, slender red-backed salamanders often are the most common salamanders where they live. The young of this species have no separate aquatic stage. They adopt their parents' terrestrial lifestyle as soon as they hatch.

RED, ORANGE, OR YELLOW STRIPE ON THE BACK

UNDERSIDE MOTTLED LIKE SALT AND PEPPER

SOMETIMES HAS NO STRIPE AND IS CALLED LEAD-BACK SALAMANDER

Northern Slimy Salamander

Plethodon glutinosus LENGTH 4.75–6.75 in (12–17 cm) • HABITAT Wooded ravines, hillsides, woodlands • RANGE Southern New England to Illinois, south to Alabama and Georgia • FOOD Invertebrates

As its scientific name, *glutinosus*, suggests, the Northern Slimy Salamander is a sticky species. This salamander secretes a gluelike fluid through its skin that really puts the "slime" in "slimy." There are many different species of slimy salamanders in the eastern United States. The Northern Slimy Salamander occupies the northernmost range of the group. This species also has an isolated population in New Hampshire.

BACK IS COVERED WITH SMALL WHITE FLECKS.

SIDES HAVE LARGE WHITE, GRAY, OR YELLOW SPOTS.

BODY IS SHINY BLACK.

Red-cheeked Salamander

Plethodon jordani LENGTH 3.5–5 in (9–13 cm) ▪ HABITAT Humid coniferous and hardwood forests ▪ RANGE Southern Appalachian Mountains ▪ FOOD Worms, insects, spiders, other invertebrates

MOST RED-CHEEKED SALAMANDERS

live along the border between Tennessee and North Carolina. Similar species range north into Virginia and West Virginia and south into South Carolina and Georgia. This woodland species makes its home in leaf and needle litter, rotting logs, and bark and beneath rocks. These salamanders don't need a water source because the forest is humid, but if they start feeling dry, they will move into burrows underground to stay moist. They also head underground when ground temperatures drop. Females lay their eggs underground. When the eggs hatch, the young stay deep in the soil until the following summer.

AMPHIB file!

Red-cheeked Salamanders live in an area with different salamander species that have overlapping ranges. These coexisting salamanders are not territorial, and their habitats are similar. Though they compete for the same food resources, this system seems to work for them.

GRAY OR BLACK BODY

RED, ORANGE, OR YELLOW CHEEK PATCHES

SOMETIMES HAS RED LEGS

10s spotters

EXPERT'S CIRCLE

DON'T BE FOOLED The **IMITATOR SALAMANDER** (*Desmognathus imitator*) belongs to the dusky salamander group, but it imitates the Red-cheeked Salamander with its yellow, orange, or reddish cheek patches. That's because the Red-cheeked has skin toxins, and enemies stay away. The Imitator lives in the southern Appalachians, mostly inside Great Smoky Mountains National Park.

FROGS AND TOADS

Eastern Spadefoot

Scaphiopus holbrookii LENGTH 1.7–2.2 in (4–6 cm) ▪ HABITAT Woods, brushlands, farmland ▪ RANGE Southern New England to Florida, west to Texas, north to Illinois, Indiana, Ohio ▪ FOOD Insects, other invertebrates

LIKE ALL SPADEFOOTS, Eastern Spadefoots come with their own digging tools. They have a small, horny "spade" on each hind foot that they use for digging their underground burrows in loose sand or soil. The Spadefoot is sometimes called a toad, although it's not a true toad. It has vertical pupils and lacks the bumpy skin and visible paratoid glands behind the eyes that toads have. The Eastern Spadefoot stays underground unless it's driven from its burrow by flooding from a lot of rain. The male's advertisement call, used to call out to potential mates during breeding time, sounds something like the squawk of a young crow.

AMPHIB file!

Express frogs! Eastern Spadefoots often mate in very temporary pools of water where the females lay their eggs. Because the water could dry up at any time, the eggs hatch in only a few days. And the tadpoles can morph into frogs in as few as two weeks!

10s spotters

MAY HAVE 2 LIGHT LINES RUNNING DOWN THE BACK

OLIVE, BROWN, OR BLACK BODY

SMALL, HORNY "SPADE" ON HIND FEET

What do you get if you cross a frog and a dog?

A croaker spaniel!

Laugh Out Loud!

Plains Spadefoot

Spea bombifrons LENGTH 1.25–2.5 in (3–6 cm) ▪ HABITAT Shrublands, grasslands, farmland, arid areas near water ▪ RANGE South-central Canada through central U.S., mainly east of Rocky Mountains ▪ FOOD Insects, other invertebrates

AMPHIB file!

The Plains Spadefoot takes advantage of warm temperatures during heavy rains. It leaves its burrow and comes to the surface, heading to wet areas where it gathers in a group to call and breed.

THE PLAINS SPADEFOOT burrows backward into the soil, using its spades. These wedge-shaped growths on its hind feet are covered in keratin, the same protein found in hair, fingernails, and hooves. The Plains Spadefoot comes out at night to forage. In hot weather, it burrows deeper to stay cool and moist. In cold weather, it burrows down even farther to get below the level of the frost.

LARGE BUMP BETWEEN EYES

4 LIGHT LINES ON BACK; MIDDLE ONES MAY FORM HOURGLASS.

BLACK WEDGE ON HIND FEET

BODY IS GREENISH, BROWN, OR GRAY.

Western Spadefoot

Spea hammondii LENGTH 1.5–2.5 in (4–6 cm) ▪ HABITAT Grassy areas, scrublands, mixed woodlands with sand and gravel ▪ RANGE Northern California through Central Valley and foothills to Baja California, Mexico ▪ FOOD Insects, worms, other invertebrates

USING ITS SPADES, the Western Spadefoot digs a burrow that creates a home with constant temperature and humidity. The frog spends most of its time there, coming to the surface mainly to find a mate. The male calls to females while floating on surface vegetation in water. The call, a short, loud trill, repeated over and over, has been compared to a short snore.

HIND FEET HAVE WEDGE-SHAPED SPADES.

DARK BLOTCHES ON BACK

LIGHT STRIPES ON BACK

OLIVE, BROWN, OR GRAY BODY

American Bullfrog

Lithobates catesbeianus LENGTH 3.5–6 in (9–15 cm) • HABITAT Nearly any body of standing or slow-moving water • RANGE Southeastern Canada and eastern U.S., introduced into West • FOOD Insects, other invertebrates, small vertebrates

FOR MANY PEOPLE, the word "frog" makes them think of the American Bullfrog, with its bright gold bulging eyes, wide froggy smile, and familiar *jug-o-rum* call. North America's largest native frog, the bullfrog can make a meal of anything it can grab with its tongue and stuff into its huge mouth with its front feet. Prey even includes birds and other bullfrogs. When grabbed by a predator, this frog lets out a loud, catlike wail. The American Bullfrog has been introduced to areas outside of where it normally lives. Local frog species suffer from the presence of the large, aggressive bullfrog—a very good example of an invasive species.

AMPHIB file!

You can tell a female from a male bullfrog by the size of the tympanum, or eardrum. In a female, the tympanum is about the same size as the eye. In the male, it's a lot larger than the eye.

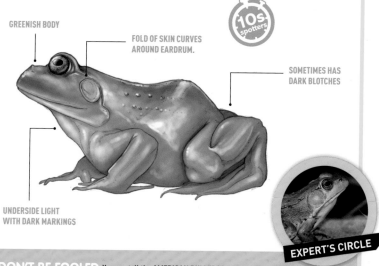

GREENISH BODY

FOLD OF SKIN CURVES AROUND EARDRUM.

SOMETIMES HAS DARK BLOTCHES

10s spotters

UNDERSIDE LIGHT WITH DARK MARKINGS

EXPERT'S CIRCLE

DON'T BE FOOLED You can tell the **AMERICAN BULLFROG** from the similar Green Frog *(Lithobates clamitans)* by the lack of a ridge that the Green Frog shows along its sides. The bullfrog has a smaller ridge that wraps around its tympanum, or eardrum.

Pickerel Frog

Lithobates palustris LENGTH 1.7–3 in (4–8 cm) • HABITAT
Woodland streams, ponds, lakes, meadows, swamps • RANGE
Southeastern Canada and eastern U.S., except extreme Southeast • FOOD
Insects, other invertebrates

THE DOUBLE ROW of rectangular blotches down the middle of its back is a good way to tell a Pickerel Frog from the closely related leopard frogs, which have roundish or oval spots on their backs. The Pickerel Frog secretes a toxin through its skin that makes it taste yucky to some predators. This toxin can also kill other frogs that are put in a closed habitat with Pickerel Frogs, like a terrarium. When many frogs are brumating in mucky pond and stream bottoms, the Pickerel may be out and about even if the pond has iced over.

LIGHT JAW STRIPE

2 ROWS OF RECTANGULAR BLOTCHES ON BACK

YELLOW FOLD ON SIDES

TAN BODY

10S. spotters

Create different kinds of amphibian eggs from a sheet of bubble wrap. You'll also need scissors, a permanent marker, tape, and some twigs.

1. Mark dots in the center of each bubble in the bubble wrap to mimic eggs.
2. Cut a 6-inch square to represent the raft of eggs laid by the female Green Frog.
3. Cut a 3-inch by 4-inch (7.5- by 10-cm) strip and tape it around a twig to show what Wood Frog eggs look like attached to vegetation.
4. Cut a single strip of bubbles to imitate American Toad eggs, which are laid in water in a long strand, like pearls.

Laugh Out Loud!

Why did the frog say "Meow!"?

It was learning a foreign language!

Northern Leopard Frog

Lithobates pipiens LENGTH 2–3.5 in (5–9 cm) ◦ HABITAT Fresh
and brackish bodies of water with dense vegetation ◦ RANGE Central and
eastern Canada, northern United States; introduced into West ◦ FOOD
Invertebrates, amphibians, snakes, small mammals

HIGH SCHOOL KIDS used to meet leopard
frogs at school. The frogs were used to teach
biology. Today, there are fewer of these frogs
because of habitat loss and pollution, among
other reasons. The Northern Leopard Frog gets
its common name from the roundish dark spots
on its back and legs. This species can tolerate
both fresh and brackish (slightly salty) water. It
can live from sea level to 11,000 feet (3,350 m). The
male's call is a deep, growly snore, often followed
by clucking noises, like a chicken. He repeats
his "theme song" over and over, with a break of
several seconds in between each one.

The Northern Leopard Frog
often leaves the water in
summer to travel to grassy
areas. This habit has given it
the nickname "meadow frog."

10s spotters

2 OR 3 ROWS OF SPOTS
BETWEEN BACK RIDGES

BROWN OR GREEN BODY

LIGHT LINE ON
UPPER JAW

EXPERT'S CIRCLE

DON'T BE FOOLED The range of **THE SOUTHERN LEOPARD FROG**
(*Lithobates sphenocephalus*) more or less ends where the range of the Northern Leopard
Frog begins, but they do overlap a bit. The Southern Leopard Frog has a pointier snout than the Northern
and a light spot in the middle of its tympanum, or ear drum.

Wood Frog

Lithobates sylvaticus LENGTH 1.3–2.75 in (3.3–7 cm) •
HABITAT Woodlands, grasslands, tundra with temporary or permanent
water sources • RANGE Much of northern North America to southern
Appalachians in the East • FOOD Insects, spiders, slugs, worms

THE HARDY WOOD FROG lives farther north than any other reptile or amphibian in North America. Its range extends all the way beyond the Arctic Circle! The breeding season for this species starts so early in some areas that ice may still be on ponds when the frogs emerge from brumation. After mating, the frogs don't hang around. They return quickly to their homes in burrows or under leaves. In summer, the species may wander very far from water. The Wood Frog's black mask sets it apart from other closely related frogs. It also has a prominent ridge extending from each eye and down its back. Female Wood Frogs can be twice as big as the males.

→ **LISTEN FOR THIS**
The male **WOOD FROG** has a call that has been described as a raspy, ducklike quack. The male produces it with not one, but two, vocal sacs. It's loud if you're nearby, but the sound doesn't travel very far through the air.

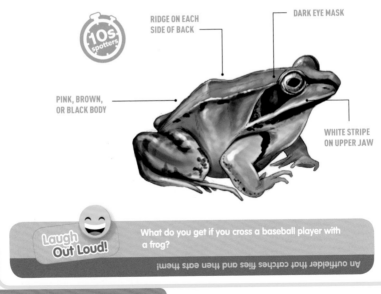

10s spotters

RIDGE ON EACH
SIDE OF BACK

DARK EYE MASK

PINK, BROWN,
OR BLACK BODY

WHITE STRIPE
ON UPPER JAW

Laugh Out Loud!
What do you get if you cross a baseball player with a frog?

An outfielder that catches flies and then eats them!

California Red-legged Frog

Rana draytonii LENGTH 1.5–5 in (4–18 cm) · HABITAT Ponds, pools, quiet streams, wet meadows · RANGE Central to Southern California · FOOD Invertebrates, small amphibians, mammals

THE CALIFORNIA RED-LEGGED FROG isn't a fan of hot weather. It would rather stay in cool, moist spaces. To escape high heat, it will rest in leaf litter and mammal burrows. In the breeding season, males call to females with a series of grunts that ends in a growl. This species used to roam over a large part of California but now is found in a much smaller area. It suffers from habitat loss and is also losing out to the aggressive American Bullfrog, an introduced species in California. It is now listed as threatened. Until recently, this frog was considered a subspecies of *Rana aurora*, the Northern Red-legged Frog.

AMPHIB file!

The American writer Mark Twain made this handsome amphibian very famous when he wrote about it in his short story "The Celebrated Jumping Frog of Calaveras County." The jumping competition Twain described is still held each May in Calaveras County, California.

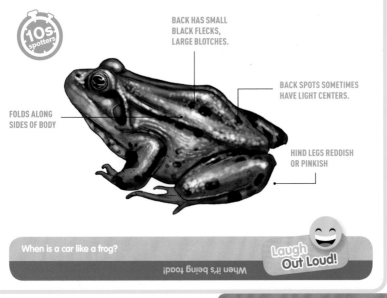

10s. spotters

BACK HAS SMALL BLACK FLECKS, LARGE BLOTCHES.

BACK SPOTS SOMETIMES HAVE LIGHT CENTERS.

FOLDS ALONG SIDES OF BODY

HIND LEGS REDDISH OR PINKISH

When is a car like a frog?

When it's being toad!

Laugh Out Loud!

Morphing Frogs

AS AMPHIBIANS, most frogs lead double lives, the way many salamander species also do. After hatching from an egg, they are aquatic fishlike creatures known as tadpoles until they change, or morph, into adult frogs that can also live on land. The whole process, called metamorphosis, can take about 16 weeks. Sometimes it is much quicker, especially when tadpoles live in temporary pools of water that might dry up. Most frog species breed and lay eggs in water, but a few lay eggs in muddy or moist places, and the tadpole changes into a frog before hatching from the egg. Toads are frogs that live mainly on land, but they, too, start their lives as tadpoles. Here you can see the frog morphing process, from egg to land-based hopper. You might be able to see these changes for yourself if you visit the same pond at different times of the year.

Eggs are laid in a big mass, often attached to plants in water.

The eggs hatch into tadpoles.

At 4 to 7 weeks, limbs begin to emerge, and the head begins to enlarge.

At 9 to 12 weeks, the tadpole begins to lose its tail.

At 12 to 16 weeks, the rest of the tail disappears, completing the transformation into an adult frog.

Eastern Narrow-mouthed Frog

Gastrophryne carolinensis LENGTH 0.75–1.25 in (2–3 cm) • HABITAT Moist cover near bodies of water • RANGE Southeastern U.S. • FOOD Ants, other small insects

AMPHIBfile!

The female Eastern Narrow-mouthed Frog lays her eggs as a film on the surface of water. The eggs take only a few days to hatch into tadpoles.

THE CHUBBY LITTLE Eastern Narrow-mouthed Frog has a small, pointy head with a very tiny mouth, so it doesn't try to eat supersize insects. It chooses mainly tiny insects, such as ants, for its meals. This little frog hides by day under natural and artificial cover, coming out at night to forage. It will often sit near the opening of an anthill and wait for its food to deliver itself!

10s spotters

LIGHT STRIPE ON SIDES

FOLD OF SKIN BEHIND EYES

GRAY, BROWN, OR RED BODY

POINTY HEAD

Western Narrow-mouthed Frog

Gastrophryne olivacea LENGTH 0.8–1.5 in (2–4 cm) • HABITAT Moist ground in leaf litter, under rocks • RANGE South-central U.S., Nebraska to Texas, reaching to Arizona • FOOD Ants, other small insects

LIKE THE EASTERN NARROW-MOUTHED FROG, the Western Narrow-mouthed Frog has a small oval body and pointy head with a fold of skin behind the eyes. It also hides in damp places and prefers the same kind of food, feeding mainly on ants. The Western Narrow-mouthed Frog sometimes shelters in rodent, reptile, and spider burrows.

10s spotters

POINTY HEAD

FOLD OF SKIN BEHIND EYES

TAN, GRAY, OR OLIVE BODY

MAY HAVE BLACK SPOTS ON BACK

American Toad

Anaxyrus americanus LENGTH 2–3.5 in (5–9 cm) • HABITAT Diverse habitats, from mountains to sea level, with moist shelter • RANGE Eastern Canada and U.S. • FOOD Insects, other invertebrates

THE AMERICAN TOAD has a lightning-fast tongue that can zap a fly in the blink of an eye! Common in the eastern United States and Canada, this toad has warty skin and short limbs with long toes. It can live in many different kinds of habitats. At breeding time, the male visits a shallow pool of water. He inflates his throat sac and calls his invitation to the females with a long, cricketlike trill. The larger females lay up to 20,000 eggs in the water in long, double strands that have a separation between each egg. A dwarf subspecies of American Toad, *Anaxyrus americanus charlesmithi*, measures about one-third shorter.

MAKE THIS!

If you have an extra clay flowerpot—even a broken one—you have a toad house!

1. Find a quiet area of your yard near vegetation and away from any dogs.
2. Put the flowerpot on its side and dig a pot-shaped hole several inches deep in the ground.
3. Bury the pot on its side about halfway, so there's an opening for the frog to get in. Put an inch of soil inside.
4. Add dried leaves on top of the soil.
5. Fill the flowerpot saucer with water and place it nearby.
6. Wait for a toad to move in!

You can camouflage the pot by covering it with waterproof green paint or by gluing pebbles on it.

10s spotters

SPOTS WITH WARTS ON BACK

PARATOID GLAND IS SEPARATE FROM HEAD CREST.

OLIVE, BROWN, OR RED BODY

What kinds of shoes do frogs like?

Open-toad sandals!

Laugh Out Loud!

Great Plains Toad

Anaxyrus cognatus LENGTH 2–3 in (5–8 cm) ▪ HABITAT Grasslands, brushlands, farmland ▪ RANGE Great Plains from southern Canada south to U.S. Southwest ▪ FOOD Insects

FARMERS LIKE THE GREAT PLAINS TOAD—a lot! The nocturnal amphibian likes to chow down on tasty cutworms, which are moth caterpillars that feed on and destroy crops. When this toad feels threatened, it goes into defense mode. It inflates itself to become even bigger and closes its eyes, sometimes lowering its head. If a predator grabs it, the toad secretes a toxin from glands behind its eyes. The toxin feels fiery in the predator's mouth.

GRAY, OLIVE, OR BROWN BODY

BODY HAS DARK BLOTCHES WITH LIGHT BORDERS.

TWO BONY RIDGES CALLED CRANIAL CRESTS FORM A "V" BETWEEN THE EYES.

10s. spotters

Red-spotted Toad

Anaxyrus punctatus LENGTH 1.5–3 in (4–8 cm) ▪ HABITAT Desert, rocky areas, grasslands, scrublands, woodlands, arroyos ▪ RANGE Southeastern California to central Texas ▪ FOOD Insects

THE FLATTENED HEAD AND BODY of the Red-spotted Toad allow it to hide among rocks and crevices. Its color blends with the environment of its Southwestern range. During the spring and summer breeding season, males gather at the edge of shallow pools. Their vocal sacs expand as they make high, trilling calls. These noises sound more musical than the calls of many other toads.

ROUND PAROTOID GLANDS

10s. spotters

HEAD AND BACK FLAT

GREENISH TO GRAYISH-BROWN BODY

BODY HAS SMALL, REDDISH WARTS.

Oak Toad

Anaxyrus quercicus LENGTH 0.75–1.3 in (2–3 cm) • HABITAT Sandy and loose soils in pine and oak scrub • RANGE Along coast from southeastern Virginia to Texas, into northeastern Alabama • FOOD Insects

THE OAK TOAD IS THE SMALLEST TOAD in North America, but that doesn't keep it from being noticed. At breeding pools in the spring, swarms of these mini-toads create a big racket with their high-pitched calls that sound like peeping chicks. Unlike many nocturnal toad species, the Oak Toad hunts for insects by day and hides the rest of the time, except during breeding season.

LIGHT STRIPE ON BACK

LIGHT GRAY TO BLACK BODY

FINE BUMPS ON BODY

Southern Toad

Anaxyrus terrestris LENGTH 1.5–3 in (4–8 cm) • HABITAT Sandy areas, edges of ponds and lakes, wooded areas, yards • RANGE Coastal plain from southern Virginia through Florida, along Gulf Coast to Louisiana • FOOD Insects, other small invertebrates

THE SOUTHERN TOAD is one gnarly amphibian! It has warts galore, as well as knobs, or bumps, on its head and even tubercles, small fleshy projections, between its warts. To attract a mate, the Southern Toad inflates its rounded vocal sac to the max, creating a high-pitched, piercing trill. The female deposits her eggs in double strands in shallow water, which sometimes dries up before the eggs can hatch.

CREST ON HEAD HAS KNOBS.

CAN HAVE STRIPE DOWN BACK

BROWN, REDDISH, OR BLACK BODY

Cane Toad

Rhinella marina **LENGTH 4–6 in (10–15 cm)** • **HABITAT Cane fields, open forests, grazing lands, parks, gardens, yards** • **RANGE Southern Texas to South America, introduced into Florida** • **FOOD Invertebrates, vertebrates, plant matter**

THE CANE TOAD was brought into the southern United States from Central and South America to protect valuable sugar cane fields. It munches on the beetle larvae that feed on the plants and destroy them. The toad did its job well, but it didn't stay put in the cane fields—no surprise there! Now the huge toad has made a home in Florida, where the population grew from toads that escaped from animal dealers. Not only does the Cane Toad compete with native frogs for food, it eats them very easily with its enormous mouth!

AMPHIB file!

Cane Toads have another unfair advantage over native frogs and toads: They can reproduce year-round. Females lay thousands of eggs at a time. The eggs hatch into mega-tadpoles that compete for food with tadpoles of other species, including the native Southern Toad.

DANGER!

Cane Toads secrete toxins from large glands behind their eyes, called paratoid glands. The toxin poisons an animal by affecting its heart and central nervous system. Victims sometimes include curious dogs and cats, so keep an eye on your outdoor pets if you live in a Cane Toad area.

10s spotters

BROWN BODY

OFTEN HAS DARK MOTTLING

LARGE, PITTED GLAND BEHIND EYES

Eastern Cricket Frog

Acris crepitans LENGTH 0.6–1.5 in (1.5–4 cm) ◦ HABITAT Shallow, sunny water with plants; quiet-stream banks ◦ RANGE Southern New York to Mississippi River, except Appalachians, Atlantic coastal plain, and peninsular Florida ◦ FOOD Insects

THE EASTERN CRICKET FROG belongs to a genus of treefrogs that doesn't spend a lot of time in the trees. It lacks toe pads on its feet, doesn't climb very much, and hops like a cricket to get where it needs to go. The call of this species is a high-pitched, rapid clicking that sounds like a bunch of marbles being shaken in a bag.

→ **LOOK FOR THIS**
The **EASTERN CRICKET FROG** comes in a wide range of colors and patterns. To tell them apart from other cricket frogs and treefrogs, you often have to look for the ragged stripe on the thighs or the large amount of webbing between the toes.

TRIANGLE BETWEEN EYES

RAGGED STRIPES ON BACK OF THIGHS

GREENISH BROWN, YELLOW, RED, OR BLACK BODY

Southern Cricket Frog

Acris gryllus LENGTH 0.6–1.25 in (1.5–3 cm) ◦ HABITAT Bogs, swamps, ponds, lakes, streams ◦ RANGE Southeastern Virginia through Florida and Gulf Coast to Mississippi River ◦ FOOD Insects, spiders

POINTY HEAD

DARK TRIANGLE BETWEEN EYES

THIS SMALL, WARTY FROG lacks toe pads, so it doesn't climb as well as treefrogs do. It usually sticks pretty close to the edges of ponds, lakes, and slow-moving streams. Its call sounds somewhat like marbles clicking together in a bag and is slower than the call of the Eastern Cricket Frog. Toward the end of the breeding season, calling males may attack each other as mates become scarce.

MAY HAVE BROWN TO ORANGE STRIPE DOWN BACK

LONG BACK LEGS

STRAIGHT LINE ON BACK OF THIGHS

Green Treefrog

Hyla cinerea **LENGTH** 1.25–2.25 in (3–6 cm) ▪ **HABITAT** Permanent bodies of water with vegetation ▪ **RANGE** Delaware to Florida Keys and along Gulf Coast to Texas; north through Arkansas to Illinois ▪ **FOOD** Insects, spiders

→ LOOK FOR THIS
If you live in **GREEN TREEFROG** territory, you might want to check out your porch lights at night. These amphibians are known to hang out on windows and doors to catch insects attracted to the lights.

AT BREEDING TIME, hundreds or even thousands of Green Treefrogs move into ponds and form a big chorus. They cling to plants sticking out of the water and sing in different pitches. Their basic call sounds a bit like a cowbell: *quonk, quonk, quonk.* Large, sticky toe pads make the Green Treefrog a champion tree climber, where its color helps it blend in.

GREEN, YELLOW, OR GRAYISH BODY

OFTEN HAS GOLD FLECKS ON BACK

OFTEN HAS WHITE OR YELLOWISH STRIPE ON SIDE

Gray Treefrog

Hyla versicolor **LENGTH** 1.25–2 in (3–5 cm) ▪ **HABITAT** Trees and shrubs in or near water ▪ **RANGE** Southeastern Canada, northeastern U.S. south to Texas ▪ **FOOD** Insects

IF YOU SAW A GRAY TREEFROG and thought it might be a toad, you wouldn't be the only one. With a squat body, wide mouth, and warty skin, it doesn't look very much like your average treefrog. This nocturnal species usually hangs out in low trees and shrubs, coming to the ground only to call and find a mate in spring and summer.

DARK-EDGED LIGHT SPOT UNDER EYE

ROUGH SKIN ON BACK

GRAY, GREEN, OR ALMOST WHITE BODY

THIGHS YELLOWISH ORANGE UNDERNEATH

Cuban Treefrog

Osteopilus septentrionalis **LENGTH 1.5–5.5 in (4–14 cm)** ·
HABITAT Any steady source of moisture, including cellars, drains, potted plants · **RANGE Southern Florida** · **FOOD Insects, spiders, frogs**

THE CUBAN TREEFROG came to the United States from Cuba about a hundred years ago. It probably hitched a ride here, possibly traveling on floating debris to the Florida Keys. It is now the largest treefrog in the United States. The species has enormous, cartoonish toe pads on its large feet. It doesn't need a lot of moisture to live and can even be found among the moist leaves of well-watered potted plants. The Cuban Treefrog's call is a snarly rasp that kind of makes it sound like it's mad. This alien species competes with native species for habitat and food and even eats other frogs.

→ **LOOK FOR THIS**
CUBAN TREEFROGS take advantage of unusual sources of food made possible by living in urban areas. You can find this nocturnal species on lighted billboards that provide a diverse buffet of insects attracted to the bright lights.

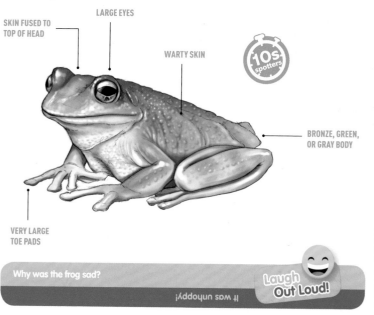

SKIN FUSED TO TOP OF HEAD

LARGE EYES

WARTY SKIN

10S. spotters

BRONZE, GREEN, OR GRAY BODY

VERY LARGE TOE PADS

Why was the frog sad?

It was unhoppy!

Laugh Out Loud!

Spring Peeper

Pseudacris crucifer **LENGTH 0.25–1.25 in (0.6–3 cm)** • **HABITAT Wooded areas near permanent or temporary ponds or pools** • **RANGE Southeastern Canada and eastern U.S.** • **FOOD Insects, spiders, other invertebrates**

THE SPRING PEEPER is named for the sound it makes. While one frog may make a peep with its high-pitched call, a pond full of males competing for mates sings a chorus of peeps to announce the arrival of spring. If you live in the South, you may even hear peepers calling in winter. A peek into a breeding pool may reveal single eggs or small clusters of them attached to vegetation or other underwater objects. In many places, peepers seem to disappear for the rest of the year, making it very difficult to catch a glimpse of the signature X on their back.

MAKE THIS!

"Stop the Squish" Info Poster

In early spring, male frogs gather in ponds and temporary pools to find mates that will lay eggs there. On the way to and from the water, frogs sometimes have to cross roads or paths—and they don't look both ways! If you know a place where frogs—or perhaps salamanders—are in danger from drivers, bikers, or walkers, make a poster that explains what's going on. Ask if you can put up a temporary "Stop the Squish!" sign or make a presentation to your classmates.

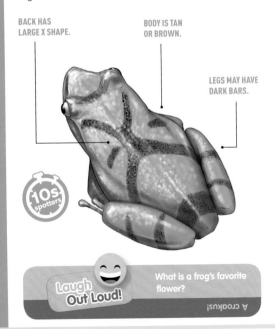

BACK HAS LARGE X SHAPE.

BODY IS TAN OR BROWN.

LEGS MAY HAVE DARK BARS.

10s spotters

Laugh Out Loud!

What is a frog's favorite flower?

A croakus!

Pacific Treefrog

Pseudacris regilla LENGTH 0.75–2 in (2–5 cm) • HABITAT Forests, grasslands, shrublands, farmland near water • RANGE Southern British Columbia through California, east to Montana and Nevada • FOOD Insects, other invertebrates

COMING TO A THEATER NEAR YOU! Because many movies and TV shows are filmed in California, the voice of the Pacific Treefrog is often heard when nighttime nature sounds are required in a scene—even when the scene is set elsewhere in the world! This treefrog is common in many different habitats from sea level to more than 11,000 feet (3,300 m). But it mostly stays on the ground, sticking close to shrubs and grasses near water. It also lives on some coastal islands.

DARK LINE THROUGH EYE

OFTEN HAS DARK BLOTCHES

MALE HAS GRAY THROAT.

GREEN, TAN, RED, OR BLACK BODY

Midland Chorus Frog

Pseudacris triseriata LENGTH 0.75–1.5 in (2–4 cm) • HABITAT Grassy areas, swamps, woodlands, farmland, urban areas • RANGE Western New York and Michigan south to Tennessee • FOOD Invertebrates

CHORUS FROGS DON'T LIKE TO SING SOLO— the bigger the group they can sing in, the better. The advertisement call of the male Midland Chorus Frog sounds like a thumb scraping across the small-tooth end of a comb. Males call while sitting on top of plants on the surface of ponds. Otherwise, these tiny frogs are pretty hard to spot. The dark stripes on their back help them blend into their surroundings.

GREEN-GRAY, BROWN, OR RED BODY

DARK STRIPE THROUGH EYE RUNS DOWN SIDE.

LIGHT STRIPE ALONG UPPER JAW

FEET HAVE NO TOE PADS OR WEBBING.

3 DARK STRIPES ON BACK

REPTILE & AMPHIB REPORT
The Invaders!

African Clawed Frog

Xenopus laevis

LENGTH: 2–2.5 in (5–6 cm)

HABITAT: Natural and artificial bodies of standing and slow-moving water

RANGE: California; reported in other states

FOOD: Aquatic invertebrates and vertebrates

FACT: It is against the law to sell or own this frog in a number of states.

IGUANAS ARE NATIVE TO THE TROPICS OF MEXICO, CENTRAL AMERICA, AND THE CARIBBEAN. SOME KINDS HAVE BECOME INVASIVE IN FLORIDA.

Burmese Python

Python bivittatus
LENGTH: 7–12 ft (2–4 m)
HABITAT: Swamps, canals, wooded and open areas
RANGE: Southern Florida
FOOD: Mammals, birds, alligators
FACT: A female python captured in Florida carried 87 eggs.

Nile Monitor

Varanus niloticus
LENGTH: 5–7 ft (1.5–2 m)
HABITAT: Swamps, banks of canals, lakes, rivers; suburban and urban areas
RANGE: Southern Florida
FOOD: Crabs, fish, amphibians, reptiles, birds, mammals, eggs
FACT: Nile Monitors sometimes enter homes through doggie doors!

SPECIES THAT ARE brought into an area and are not native to that place are called introduced or alien species. They can be plants or animals. They are known as invasive species if they hog space and resources. Many introduced reptiles and amphibians came to North America through the pet trade, often from tropical countries. These animals escaped—or were dumped by people tired of taking care of them. If these invaders like the habitat and the food, they can be so successful that they threaten native species. The Nile Monitor, a ginormous African lizard that can be as long as some cars, thrives in southern Florida. It eats Burrowing Owls, sea turtles, and alligators. Also in southern Florida, the Burmese Python takes over other predators' territories. The African Clawed Frog harms native wildlife by spreading a deadly fungus.

Quick ID Guide

QUICK! What's that little creature flashing like lightning across your porch? The images on these pages will help you identify it at a glance. These profiles give examples of species in the main families of reptiles and amphibians in this book. Be sure to check out other species in each family on the pages listed with them. Grab your pad and pencil to make notes, so you can identify the next critter that zooms across your porch, lumbers across the road at a turtle's pace, or slithers out of your garden!

REPTILES

CROCODILIANS

American Crocodile
Crocodylidae: 14

ALLIGATORIDAE

American Alligator
Alligatoridae: 15

TURTLES

Snapping Turtle
Chelydridae: 16–17

TURTLES

Loggerhead Musk Turtle
Kinosternidae: 18–20

Northwestern Pond Turtle
Emydidae: 21–30

Mojave Desert Tortoise
Testudinae: 31

TURTLES

Loggerhead Sea Turtle
Cheloniidae: 32–35

Leatherback Sea Turtle
Dermochelyidae: 36

Smooth Softshell
Trionychidae: 37

LIZARDS

Western Banded Gecko
Eublepharidae: 40

Reef Gecko
Sphaerodactylidae: 40

Madagascan Day Gecko
Gekkonidae: 41

LIZARDS

Green Anole
Dactyloidae: 42

Eastern Collared Lizard
Crotaphytidae: 43

Jackson's Chameleon
Chamaeleonidae: 47

LIZARDS

Desert Iguana
Iguanidae: 48–49

Zebra-tailed Lizard
Phrynosomatidae: 50–57

Southern Alligator Lizard
Anguidae: 58–59

LIZARDS

Gila Monster
Helodermatidae: 60

Marbled Whiptail
Teiidae: 61–63

Common Five-lined Skink
Scincidae: 64–65

LIZARDS

Little Brown Skink
Sphenomorphidae: 66

Florida Wormlizard
Rhineuridae: 67

SNAKES

Western Threadsnake
Leptotyphlopidae: 68

SNAKES

Northern Rubber Boa
Boidae: 69–70

North American Racer
Colubridae: 71–80

Common Wormsnake
Dipsadidae: 81–83

SNAKES

Plain-bellied Watersnake
Natricidae: 84–96

Arizona Coralsnake
Elapidae: 97

Eastern Copperhead
Viperidae: 98–104

AMPHIBIANS

SALAMANDERS

Eastern Hellbender
Cryptobranchidae: 105

Common Mudpuppy
Proteidae: 106

Lesser Siren
Sirenidae: 107

Two-toed Amphiuma
Amphiumidae: 108

Red-spotted Newt
Salamandridae: 109

Blue-spotted Salamander
Ambystomatidae: 110–112

California Giant Salamander
Dicamptodontidae: 113

Green Salamander
Plethodontidae: 114–124

Eastern Spadefoot
Scaphiopodidae: 125–126

American Bullfrog
Ranidae: 127–131

Eastern Narrow-mouthed
Frog
Microhylidae: 134

American Toad
Bufonidae: 135–138

Eastern Cricket Frog
Hylidae: 139–143

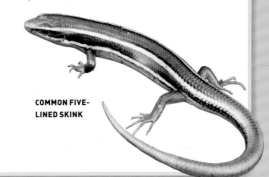

**COMMON FIVE-
LINED SKINK**

Glossary

ADAPTATION: A specialized body part—like a tail or tongue—or behavior that increases the chances that an animal will survive and reproduce

ALGAE: Simple, photosynthetic organisms found mostly in water

AQUATIC: Living in water

ARID: Receiving little rain

BARBEL: A fleshy projection on the chin or throat of some turtles

BRACKISH: A mixture of salt- and freshwaters that occurs, for example, where a river enters the sea

BRUMATION: An inactive state, similar to hibernation, that some reptiles and amphibians use to survive cold winter months

CAMOUFLAGE: Skin color or pattern that helps an animal blend with its surroundings

CARAPACE: Upper part of a turtle or tortoise shell, usually composed of bone covered by very large scales called scutes

CARRION: The remains of dead animals

CHAPARRAL: A dry habitat found mostly in the West that has tangled shrubs and thorny bushes

CLUTCH: A group of eggs laid at the same time

CONCENTRIC: Circles or other shapes that share the same center

CRUSTACEAN: A mainly aquatic invertebrate animal—such as a crayfish—with a hard shell and jointed limbs

ECOLOGICAL: Concerning how living things relate to each other and to their surroundings

ECTOTHERMIC (COLD-BLOODED): Regulating body temperature by using environmental sources of heat

ENDOTHERMIC (WARM-BLOODED): Regulating body temperature using heat generated by the internal processes of the body

EXTINCT: No longer existing anywhere on Earth

FANG: A long, sharp tooth that is sometimes grooved or hollow to allow the injection of venom

FORAGE: To go out over an area in search of food

GENUS: A group of related organisms that includes one or more species

GILLS: Organs of fish and amphibian larvae (and some adults) used to extract oxygen from and excrete carbon dioxide into water

HABITAT: The natural home and surroundings of an organism

HAMMOCK: A group of trees growing on land elevated above another kind of habitat, such as hardwood trees growing in the middle of wetlands

HARDPAN: A layer of clay, usually beneath the top layer of soil, that blocks water drainage and prevents plant growth

HERBIVORE: An animal that eats plants

HIBERNATION: A deep sleep that some mammals use to survive winter conditions

INVASIVE SPECIES: A species that is not native to an area and harms native species or ecosystems

INVERTEBRATE: An animal that does not have a backbone, or vertebral column

JUVENILE: A young animal not yet capable of reproduction

LARVA: A stage of an amphibian's life after hatching from the egg in which it feeds actively to store energy for metamorphosis

LEAF LITTER: Thick layers of fallen leaves and other plant debris in which many reptiles and amphibians seek shelter and forage for food

METAMORPHOSIS: The transformation of an animal from one stage in life to another, such as a tadpole becoming an adult frog or toad

NATIVE SPECIES: A species that occurs naturally in an area

NONNATIVE SPECIES: A species that does not occur naturally in an area

ORGANISM: A plant, animal, or other form of life, such as a bacterium

PARATOID: Prominent gland behind the eyes of some frogs (especially toads) and salamanders that secretes a toxic substance

PLASTRON: The flat bottom part of a turtle or tortoise shell, usually composed of bone covered by very large scales called scutes

PRAIRIE: A large area of grassland

PREDATOR: An animal that hunts other animals (prey) for food

PREHENSILE: Having the ability to grasp

PREY: An animal that is hunted and killed by other animals for food

SCALE: A tough structure produced by the outer layer of skin that typically covers the body of reptiles

SECRETE: To emit a liquid substance

SPECIES: A group of related animals that can interbreed and produce fertile offspring

TADPOLE: The larva of a frog or toad

TOXIC: Unpleasant or harmful, like snake venom or some amphibian skin secretions

TRIBUTARY: A river or stream that flows into a larger river

TUNDRA: A treeless area in the Arctic or on high mountain slopes often covered with low-growing plants

VENOM: A toxic substance formed and transmitted by some animals, like snakes and bees, that is injected by biting or stinging

VENT: An area on the underside with an opening to the digestive, urinary, and reproductive tracts in amphibians and reptiles

VERTEBRA: One of the bones that composes the backbone, or vertebral column, of a vertebrate

VERTEBRATE: An animal that has a backbone, or vertebral column

FIND OUT More

WANT TO FIND OUT EVEN MORE about reptiles and amphibians? Check out these great books, websites, apps, and movies. Be sure to ask an adult to help you search the Web to find the sites listed below.

BOOKS

National Geographic Kids Mission: Sea Turtle Rescue, 2015

National Geographic Kids: Ultimate Reptilopedia, 2015

National Geographic Readers: Alligators and Crocodiles, 2015

National Geographic Readers: Frogs!, 2009

National Geographic Readers: Lizards, 2012

National Geographic Readers: Sea Turtles, 2011

National Geographic Readers: Snakes!, 2009

WEBSITES

San Diego Zoo Kids
(San Diego Zoo)
kids.sandiegozoo.org/animals/amphibians

USGS Frog Quiz
(Patuxent Wildlife Research Center)
pwrc.usgs.gov/frogquiz/

APPS

Audubon Reptiles and Amphibians—A Field Guide to North American Reptiles and Amphibians

MOVIES

BBC: *Life, Reptiles and Amphibians* (NR Documentary)

National Geographic: *Realm of the Alligator* (NR Documentary)

Index

Boldface indicates illustrations.

Artwork appearing in this book was created by Jared Travnicek.

CO = Corbis; GI = Getty Images; IS = iStockphoto; NGC = National Geographic Creative; SS = Shutterstock

Cover: Background: Shutterstock; snake: B&S Draker/ NPL/Minden Pictures; salamander: Michael Durham/Minden Pictures; sea turtle: Rich Carey/Shutterstock; chameleon: Eric Isselee/Shutterstock; back cover: Brian Lasenby/Shutterstock;1, Hal Beral/CO; 2-3. Isabelle Bonaire/AS; 4 (tp), SS/Brian Lasenby; 4 (md), SS/Malgorzata Litkowska; 4 (lo), SS/LorraineHudgins; 5 (tp), Gerold & Cynthia Merker/Visuals Unlimited; 5 (lo), SS/Jason Mintzer; 6-7, SS/Nagel Photography; 8 (tp), SS/Dmitry Naumov; 10-11, Mike Pingleton; 11 (lo), SS/Kuttelvaserova Stuchelova; 11 (tp), SS/Petr Malyshev; 12 (lo), Roy Toft/NGC; 12 (tp), SS/ Michiel de Wit; 13 (tp), SS/Francesco Ocello; 13 (md lo), SS/Sittipong; 13 (lo), SS/Sagir; 14 (tp), SS/Leonardo Gonzalez; 14 (lo), ItinerantLens/ AS; 15 (tp), SS/Heiko Kiera; 16 (tp), SS/Suthat Chaithaweesap 16 (md tp), SS/Andrea J Smith; 17, SS/Ryan M. Bolton; 18 (up), Alex Mustard/ NaturePL; 18 (lo), SS/Seth LaGrange; 19 (tp), SS/Fivespots; 19 (lo), Suzanne L. Collins/Science Source; 20 (tp), Jake Holmes/GI/IS; 21 (tp), SS/Sekar B; 21 (lo), FLPA/L. Lee Rue; 22 (tp), SS/Jay Ondreicka; 22 (lo), SS/ecliptic blue; 23 (tp), SS/Marc Parsons; 23 (lo), Rex Lisman/GI/Flickr RF;. 24, Justin Coleman; 25 (tp), Michael Redmer/GI/Visuals Unlimited; 25 (lo), SS/Bildagentur Zoonar GmbH; 26, SS/Uwe Ohse; 27 (tp), SS/ Simon_g; 27 (lo), Paulina Lenting-Smulders/GI/IS; 28 (tp), Berndneeser/ GI/IS; 28 (lo), SS/fivespots; 29 (tp), SS/Brian Lasenby; 30 (tp), Robert Powell; 30 (lo), SS/Ryan M. Bolton; 31 (tp), SS/IrinaK; 31 (lo), ArendTrent/GI/IS; 32, SS/Willyam Bradberry; 33, SS/mrHanson; 34, SS/Rich Carey; 35 (tp), Michael Patrick O'Neill/Alamy; 35 (lo), marcinhajdasz/GI/IS; 36, SS/ Stephanie Rousseau; 37 (tp), Suzanne L. & Joseph T. Collins/Science Source; 37 (lo), SS/Ryan M. Bolton; 38-39, Longjourneys/AS; 39 (tp), Mike Parry/NGC/Minden Pictures; 39 (md), davidevison/AS; 39 (lo), Michael Melford/NGC; 40 (tp), SS/Chaikom; 40 (md), SS/Matt Jeppson; 40 (lo), Barry Mansell/NPL/Minden Pictures; 41 (tp), SS/Evgeny Murtola; 41 (lo), zlikovec/GI/IS; 42 (tp), leekris/AS; 42 (lo), SS/Steve Bower; 43, SS/Malgorzata Litkowska; 44-45. Dave Hughes/GI/IS; 45 (tp), leekris/ AS; 45 (md), SS/Matt Jeppson; 45 (lo), MAK/AS; 46 (tp), SS/Jason Mintzer; 46 (lo), Jack Goldfarb/GI/Design Pics RF; 47 (tp), Mark Kostich/ GI/IS; 47 (lo), SS/Nashepard; 48 (tp), SS/Jason Mintzer; 48 (lo), SS/ SantiPhotoSS; 49, SS/Andrew Chin; 50, SS/kojihirano; 51 (tp), Robert Shantz/Alamy Stock Photo; 51 (lo), SS/tntphototravis; 52, Sally Ann Barnes/AS; 53. Lee H. Rentz; 54 (tp), SolomonCrowe/GI/IS; 54 (lo), SS/ Riegsecker; 55 (tp), SS; 55 (lo), SS/Kim Murrell; 56, SS/Lindsay Helms; 57, SS/Tom Reichner. 58 (tp), SS/Eric Rounds; 58 (lo), James Gerholdt/ GI; 59 (tp), SS/Matt Jeppson; 59 (lo), Allen Blake Sheldon/Animals Animals/Earth Scene/NGC 60, SS/Kris Wiktor; 61, Bill Gorum/Alamy Stock Photo; 62, SS/Sari ONeal; 63 (tp), Robert Shantz/Alamy; 63 (lo). SS/Martha Marks; 64 (tp), SS/Pan Xunbin; 64 (lo), SS/Wolf Mountain Images; 65 (tp), SS/Randimal; 65 (lo), Barry Mansell/NPL/Minden Pictures; 66, TW Pierson; 67, Merritt Garling; 68 (tp), SS/tranac; 68 (md tp), Patrick Briggs; 68 (lo), Larry Miller/Science Source; 69, SS/ Randimal; 70, SS/Oleg Blazhyievskyi; 71 (tp), Larry Miller/GI/Photo Researchers RM; 71 (lo), Jason Ondreicka/IS; 72 (tp), SS/JNB Photography; 72 (lo), Carlton Ward/GI/NGC; 73 (tp), SS/MattiaATH; 73 (lo), SS/Matt Jeppson; 74 (tp), Robert Hamilton/Alamy Stock Photo; 74 (lo), SS/Matt Jeppson; 75 (tp), Ian Shive/TandemStock; 75 (lo), sdbower/ AS; 76 (tp), SS/Barry Blackburn; 76 (lo), pokosuke/GI/IS; 77. SS/Jay Ondreicka; 78-79, Yvette Cardozo/GI; 78, SS/Matt Jeppson; 79 (tp), Bruce Jayne/University of Cincinnati; 79 (md), SS/Yatra; 79 (lo), Gunter Ziesler/GI; 80 (tp), Eitan Grunwald; 80 (lo), SS/Matt Jeppson; 81, Eitan Grunwald; 82 (tp), SS/Jason Mintzer; 82 (lo), SS/Ryan M. Bolton; 83 (tp), mgkuijpers/AS; 83 (lo), Robert Hamilton/Alamy; 84 (tp), SS/Martha Marks; 84 (lo), Jake Holmes/GI; 85 (tp), Steve Byland/GI; 85 (lo), SS/Jo Crebbin; 86, SS/Rusty Dodson; 87 (tp), SS/Jason Patrick Ross; 87 (lo). Ken Wray; 88-89, Jeremy Sterk/GI; 88, SS/Patrick K. Campbell; 89 (tp), Rex Lisman/GI; 89 (md rt), SS/Ryan M. Bolton; 89 (md lt), SS/voylodyon;

89 (lo), SS/Heiko Kiera; 90 (tp), Steve Ogle/GI; 90 (lo), SS/Andrew McKinney; 91, SS/Rusty Dodson; 92, Rusty Dodson/GI/ IS; 93, SS/Matt Jeppson; 94-95, DArthurBrown/GI; 95 (tp), Karl H. Switak/Science Source; 95 (md), Bianca Lavies/NGC; 95 (lo), Francois Gohier/Science Source; 96, SS/Matt Jeppson; 97 (tp), Rick&Nora Bowers/Alamy Stock Photo; 97 (lo), SS/Jay Ondreicka; 98, Jake Holmes/ GI/IS; 99, Joel Sartore/NGC; 100 (tp), Milos Manojlovic/GI/IS; 100 (lo), SS/Ryan M. Bolton; 101, AZP Worldwide/AS; 102, SS/Ryan M. Bolton; 103, Bryan/AS; 104, SS/James DeBoer; 105 (tp), SS/Acer; 105 (lo), Robert Noonan/Science Source; 106, Joel Sartore/NGC; 107, Lynda Richardson/ CO; 108 (tp), Phil A. Dotson/Science Source; 108 (lo), Nature's Images/ Science Source; 109 (tp), SS/gary powell; 109 (lo), SS/Randimal; 110 (tp), SS/James DeBoer; 110 (lo), SS/Randimal; 111 (tp), Roy Toft/NGC; 111 (lo), George Grall/NGC; 112 (tp), Kenneth M Highfill/GI/Photo Researchers RM 113, SS/Matt Knoth; 114, Byron Jorjorian/Alamy; 115 (tp), Chris Mattison/FLPA/Science Source; 115 (lo), Wikipedia Commons; 116 (tp), Steve Byland/AS; 116 (lo), David M. Dennis/Animals Animals/ Earth Scenes/NGC; 117, Gerold & Cynthia Merker/Visuals Unlimited; 118 (tp), SS/Jason Patrick Ross; 118 (lo), Ken Wray; 119, Paul Zahl/NGC; 120. David M. Dennis/Animals Animals/Earth Scenes/NGC; 121, mgkuijpers/ AS; 122, David M. Dennis/Animals Animals; 123 (tp), SS/Jason Patrick Ross; 123 (lo), SS/Ryan M. Bolton; 124 (tp), John Serrao/Science Source; 124 (lo), Martin Shields/Alamy Stock Photo; 125 (tp), SS/Rosa Jay; 125 (lo), SS/Jason Patrick Ross; 126 (tp), Roberta Olenick/GI; 126 (lo), SS/ Jason Mintzer; 127 (tp), SS/Angel DiBilio; 127 (lo), SS/Paul Reeves Photography; 128, SS/Matt Jeppson; 129 (tp), Thibaut Claeys/Alamy; 129 (lo), SS/Ryan M. Bolton; 130, Michael Durham/Minden Pictures/NGC; 131, Michael & Patricia Fogden/Minden/NGC; 132-133, SS/Matej Ziak; 133 (tp), SS/Marius Neacsa; 133 (md tp), SS/prajit48; 133 (md lt), Eric Isselee/GI/IS; 133 (md rt), Eric Isselee/GI/IS; 133 (lo), Eric Isselee/GI/IS; 134 (tp), Pierson Hill; 134 (lo), Suzanne L. Collins/Science Source; 135. SS/Tom Reichner; 136 (tp), SS/Joe Farah; 136 (lo), Earl Nelson/GI/IS; 137 (tp), Michelle Gilders/Alamy; 137 (lo), Jared Hobbs/GI; 138, SS/Chris Ison; 139 (tp), Hilton Pond Center; 139 (lo), SuperStock/AGE Fotostock; 140 (tp), SS/LorraineHudgins; 140 (lo), SS/Jay Ondreicka; 141, SS/Steve Bower; 142, Custom Life Science Images/Alamy; 143 (tp), SS/Ryan M. Bolton; 143 (lo), SS/Matt Jeppson; 144-145. hakoar/AS; 144, Tad Arensmeier/GI/Flickr Flash 145 (tp), SS/MP cz; 145 (lo), davemontreuil/ AS; 146 top row (lt), SS/Leonardo Gonzalez; (md), SS/Heiko Kiera; (rt), SS/Andrea J Smith; 146 middle row (lt), Alex Mustard/NaturePL; (md), SS/Sekar B; (rt), SS/IrinaK; 146 bottom row (lt), SS/Willyam Bradberry; (md), SS/Stephanie Rousseau; (rt), Suzanne L. & Joseph T. Collins/ Science Source; 147 top row (lt), SS/Matt Jeppson; (md), Barry Mansell/ NPL/Minden Pictures; (rt), SS/Evgeny Murtola; 147 middle top row (lt), leekris/AS; (md), SS/Malgorzata Litkowska; (rt), Mark Kostich/GI/IS; 147 middle bottom row (lt), SS/Jason Mintzer; (md), SS/kojihirano; (rt), James Gerholdt/GI; 147 bottom row (lt), SS/Kris Wiktor; (md), Bill Gorum/Alamy Stock Photo; (rt), SS/Pan Xunbin; 148 top row (lt), TW Pierson; (md), Merritt Garling; (rt), Patrick Briggs; 148 middle top row (lt), SS/Randimal; (md), Larry Miller/GI/Photo Researchers RM; (rt). Eitan Grunwald; 148 middle bottom row (lt), SS/Martha Marks; (md), Rick & Nora Bowers/Alamy Stock Photo; (rt), Jake Holmes/GI/IS; 148 bottom row (lt), Robert Noonan/Science Source; (md), Joel Sartore/NGC; (rt), Lynda Richardson/CO; 149 top row (lt), Phil A. Dotson/Science Source; (md), SS/Gary Powell; (rt), SS/James DeBoer; 149 middle top row (lt), SS/Matt Knoth; (md), Byron Jorjorian/Alamy; (rt), SS/Jason Patrick Ross; 149 middle bottom row (lt), SS/Angel DiBilio; (md), Pierson Hill; (rt), SS/Tom Reichner; 149 bottom row (lt), Hilton Pond Center; (rt), SS/Randimal; 150-151, SS/NagyDodo;154, SS/Czesznak Zsolt;Hilton Pond Center; (rt), SS/Randimal; 150-151, SS/NagyDodo;154, SS/Czesznak Zsolt; 160 (lo), SS/Kuttelvaserova Stuchelova

Copyright © 2016 National Geographic Partners, LLC

National Geographic Partners, LLC, and Potomac Global Media, LLC, would like to thank the following members of the project team: Kevin Mulroy, Barbara Brownell Grogan, Catherine Herbert Howell, Matt Propert, Robert Powell, Claire McCrea, and Tim Griffin.

Published by National Geographic Partners, LLC

Since 1888, the National Geographic Society has funded more than 12,000 research, exploration, and preservation projects around the world. The Society receives funds from National Geographic Partners LLC, funded in part by your purchase. A portion of the proceeds from this book supports this vital work. To learn more, visit www.natgeo.com/info.

For more information, visit nationalgeographic.com, call 1-800-647-5463, or write to the following address:

National Geographic Partners
1145 17th Street N.W.
Washington, D.C. 20036-4688 U.S.A.

Visit us online at
nationalgeographic.com/books

For librarians and teachers:
ngchildrensbooks.org

More for kids from National Geographic:
kids.nationalgeographic.com

For information about special discounts for bulk purchases, please contact National Geographic Books Special Sales: ngspecsales@ngs.org

For rights or permissions inquiries, please contact National Geographic Books Subsidiary Rights: ngbookrights@ngs.org

NATIONAL GEOGRAPHIC and Yellow Border Design are trademarks of the National Geographic Society, used under license.

Editorial, Design, and Production by Potomac Global Media, LLC

Art Directed by Jim Hiscott, Jr.

Designed by Project Design Company

Paperback
ISBN: 978-1-4263-2544-1

Reinforced library binding
ISBN: 978-1-4263-2545-8

Printed in China

16/RRDS/1